Sowing the Dragon's TEETH

PHILIP C. WINSLOW

Sowing the Dragon's TEETH

Land Mines

and the Global

Legacy of War

Beacon Press
BOSTON

Beacon Press
25 Beacon Street
Boston, Massachusetts 02108-2892

Beacon Press books are published under the auspices
of the Unitarian Universalist Association of Congregations.

02 01 00 99 98   8 7 6 5 4 3

Text design by Lucinda L. Hitchcock
Composition by Wilsted & Taylor Publishing Services

LIBRARY OF CONGRESS CATALOGING-IN-PUBLICATION DATA
Winslow, Philip C.
    Sowing the dragon's teeth : land mines and the global legacy of war /
Philip C. Winslow.
        p.   cm.
    "Published under the auspices of the Unitarian Universalist Association
of Congregations"—Verso t.p.
    Includes bibliographical references.
    ISBN 0-8070-5004-0 (cloth)
    ISBN 0-8070-5005-9 (paper)
    I. Title.
DT1428.W56   1997
909.82—dc21   97-2721

Seeking his sister Europa, carried off by Jupiter, [Cadmus] had strange adventures — sowing in the ground teeth of a dragon he had killed, which sprang up armed men who slew each other, all but five, who helped him to found the city of Thebes.

—BULFINCH'S MYTHOLOGY

Contents

Author's Note

The Worst War in the World

To write about land mines, I decided to focus on Angola rather than, say, Bosnia-Herzegovina (which is better known in the West these days), in part because I have grown fond of Angola and its people. I also decided on Angola because political, military, and commercial interests in several countries contributed to Angola's tragedy, and the story belongs to us all.

A bit of history may make it easier to understand the origins of Angola's disintegration, the current land mine problem, and perhaps its future course – whether the current peace, brokered by the United Nations in 1994 in Lusaka, Zambia, holds or not.

A 1974 coup d'état in Portugal ended Angolan nationalist groups' struggle to evict the former colonial power. But following their independence in 1975, Angolan fighters turned on themselves and the country slipped into civil war. Angola's oil and diamonds and the prevailing geopolitical theories of the day had already concentrated attention in Washington, Moscow, and Pretoria. Powerful forces on three continents began stirring a cauldron of war that would boil for the next nineteen years.

The war was one of the greatest follies of the long standoff between the United States and the Soviet Union. In a superpower proxy struggle that wound up benefiting no one except the world's arms manufacturers, the then-Marxist Movimento Popular de Libertação de Angola (MPLA) of President José Eduardo dos Santos was supported by Soviet military muscle and Cuban troops. The União Nacional para a Independência Total de Angola (UNITA) of rebel leader Jonas Savimbi was backed by U.S. money and arms and the formidable military machine of South Africa, whose apartheid regime was then battling South West Africa People's Organization (SWAPO) guerrillas on its northwest flank in Namibia (and inside Angola).

Finally, as the Soviet Union collapsed and the Cold War ended, so did the backing of the superpowers for the factions in Angola. Namibia won independence, the Cubans went home, most of the South Africans left, funding from Washington and Moscow began to dry up, and Angola was left largely to its own devices. Neither side lacked the wherewithal to continue fighting: abundant stocks of weapons and sources of cash to buy more through clandestine supply routes.

For brief periods between 1992 and 1994, Angola reappeared in world headlines and news broadcasts after the collapse of a peace accord between the MPLA and UNITA.

That 1991 accord had resulted in elections in September 1992. The vote, judged by the United Nations to have been generally free and fair, returned the MPLA to power. UNITA cried foul, however, and Savimbi took his guerrillas back to the bush. Thus began Angola's third war in three decades.

The fighting over the next two years was more vicious than at any time in the past. An estimated 300,000 Angolans were killed. Cities like Malange, Menongue, and Kuito became synonymous with savagery and civilian suffering on a massive scale. UNITA guerrillas besieged and indiscriminately shelled MPLA-held provincial capitals, in the case of Kuito for up to a year. Kuito residents buried their dead in back gardens and reportedly ate dogs and leaves off the trees. A Bié Province vice-governor told me afterward, "For a year the only smell was of blood, the only song was the shelling."

Television and newspapers showed pictures of some of the thousands of Angolans who had lost legs to antipersonnel mines. Superlatives and comparisons entered the news stories: the war was called "The Worst War in the World." Angola was said to be the most heavily mined country in Africa and to have the highest number of amputees per inhabitant in the world. Angola took its place in the history books alongside mine-littered countries like Cambodia, Afghanistan, northern Iraq, Somalia, Bosnia-Herzegovina, Sudan, and Mozambique. Then, for most readers and viewers in industrialized countries – where mines are produced but rarely deployed – the book on Angola was quietly closed again when the fighting tapered off. The humanitarian disaster facing ten million Angolans was left primarily to a handful of international relief organizations.

In 1994, having fought themselves to a standstill, bankrupted the treasury, and destroyed what remained of the national infrastructure, the MPLA and UNITA put pen to paper in Lusaka on another peace agreement forged with great determination by the UN. There wasn't much left to fight over, in any event: the government still controlled the northwest oil-producing regions and many provincial capitals, and UNITA still had a lock on diamond-mining areas in the northeast. Even if the will to fight had remained, both sides were finding it difficult to move around: what wasn't ruined was inaccessible because of the land mines.

The United States, which gets about 6 percent of its total oil imports from Angola, and other countries continued to urge both sides to rebuild. Hopeful signs existed. Government troops and UNITA guerrillas, slowly and behind schedule, had quartered thousands of soldiers and handed in weapons to UN peacekeepers. But the former combatants still eyed one another warily across confrontation lines. Neither side was convinced the war was over. Angolans, especially civilians, had heard the promises of peace before.

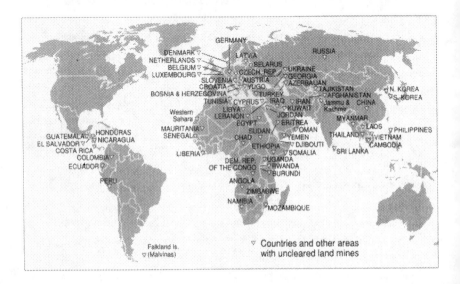

GERMANY
DENMARK
NETHERLANDS
BELGIUM
LUXEMBOURG
LATVIA
BELARUS
UKRAINE
RUSSIA
CZECH REP.
GEORGIA
SLOVENIA
CROATIA
AUSTRIA
YUGO.
AZERBAIJAN
TAJIKISTAN
BOSNIA & HERZEGOVINA
TUNISIA
CYPRUS
TURKEY
IRAQ
IRAN
AFGHANISTAN
N. KOREA
S. KOREA
Jammu &
Kashmir
CHINA
Western
Sahara
LIBYA
LEBANON
KUWAIT
EGYPT
JORDAN
MYANMAR
MAURITANIA
SENEGAL
ERITREA
SUDAN
OMAN
LAOS
PHILIPPINES
THAILAND
VIETNAM
GUATEMALA
HONDURAS
NICARAGUA
EL SALVADOR
COSTA RICA
COLOMBIA
ECUADOR
CHAD
YEMEN
CAMBODIA
ETHIOPIA
DJIBOUTI
SRI LANKA
LIBERIA
SOMALIA
DEM. REP.
OF THE CONGO
UGANDA
RWANDA
PERU
BURUNDI
ANGOLA
ZIMBABWE
NAMIBIA
MOZAMBIQUE

Falkland Is.
(Malvinas)

▽ Countries and other areas
   with uncleared land mines

Introduction

I came across land mine victims for the first time in Iran in 1988 and then again in Croatia in 1993, in the course of my job as a reporter. At the time I tended to see them as general casualties of war, rather than as victims of a particular weapon, and wrote about them, if at all, in the overall context of what was happening in each particular country.

Then, when I was covering the war in Angola in late 1993, I started actually meeting them and hearing their stories. It wasn't difficult: they were everywhere. The first one I really talked to, in the besieged Central Highlands city of Malange, was Antonio Romão, a sixty-one-year-old former soldier who had stepped on a mine as his army unit hunted rebels in the bush in 1977. Sixteen years later he was still walking on the same pair of crutches he had been given when invalided out of the army, and he still had no prospect of being fitted with an artificial leg.

As I walked with him, his untipped aluminum crutches made a hollow "thunk" each time they hit the pavement. He put what little energy he had into walking and didn't have much to say. I still remember his face and the awful rhythmic sound of his crutches on that quiet street.

Romão's condition was not unique. Every twenty minutes of every day, according to the people who try to keep track, someone, usually a civilian, is maimed or killed by a mine somewhere in the world. It happens from Egypt on the Mediterranean to Mozambique on the Indian Ocean, and from Southeast Asia to Central America. The reports seldom make the news, either in the countries where the accidents happen or abroad. But if you walk into a hospital ward in rural Angola, Somalia, the Sudan, Cambodia, or Afghanistan and ask what happened, the stories begin like this:

"I was on my way to make charcoal . . ."

"I was going out to dig cassava . . ."

"I had gone to fetch a cow that had wandered off . . ."

Then the stories trail off, usually unrecorded and unphotographed, and end with a querulous look, an unspoken question: Why did this happen to me? I was only going to . . .

Bitterness is usually left to the doctors who treat the victims in the grim wards and operating theaters of some of the world's poorest countries.

"We do not even have soap to wash the floors," an angry Dr. Joaquim Neho told me in Malange, jabbing a finger at a bare supply cupboard across from a dark room where two women lay on filthy beds. Both women had recently stepped on mines as they foraged for food or firewood; both had lost a leg. "Please tell the world not to send us land mines, but medicine and food and things we need instead," said Neho, who, like doctors in many parts of Angola, then had to perform amputations without anesthetic.

The hospital images, which on paper filter out the smell and horror of the wards, are not limited to Angola – same wounds, same stench, same fear in the eyes – just change the name of the country.

The global picture is breathtaking in scope. It is now generally believed that 110 million antipersonnel mines lie beneath the soil of seventy countries, although no one can claim to have accurate statistics. Among the victims, children pay a particularly heavy price. Intrigued by the shape or color of mines – especially the "butterfly" type that litters Afghanistan – they frequently mistake them for toys. In one hospital on the Afghan-Pakistan border, nearly a quarter of the mine victims in 1995 were children under the age of sixteen. Four years before that, one hospital in Somalia estimated that more than 74 percent of its mine victims were children. In one Angolan city, 80 percent of the mine victims over a two-year period were said to be women and children.

A 1994 United Nations report estimated that if mine laying stopped immediately, clearing the world's mines could cost $33 billion and take 1,100 years. But mine laying has not stopped: Armies and guerrilla fighters bury more than a million new mines a year, the UN says.

While the grim statistics may be revised upward or downward as time goes on, it is clear that antipersonnel mines around the world have claimed human casualties far in excess of any military utility the weapon may have had. In addition, by closing roads and taking farmland out of production, mines have contributed to the devastation of entire national economies.

During Angola's civil war, both sides laid antipersonnel mines and antitank mines without marking their location. They used (and still use) mines defensively and as weapons of terror and area-denial in order to control civilian populations. The commonly cited statistic, accepted by the UN, says that between nine million and fifteen million mines are left in Angola. But, as the experts keep saying, the estimated number of mines is likely to be both inaccurate and irrelevant. "If we knew how many mines there were, we would know where they were, and if knew where they were, we would remove them," one demining specialist told me.

The fact is that the mines exist in parts of all eighteen of Angola's provinces, buried in rich farmland, under roads and in some cases in concentric belts three kilometers (nearly two miles) deep around cities. The minefields have turned vast areas of the country into isolated enclaves that might as well be on a distant planet.

To illustrate the difficulties of post-war mine clearance, I have looked at the efforts of one charity, the Mines Advisory Group (MAG), whose headquarters is in the Lake District of England and whose Angolan teams are pulling mines in part of one province. I could have focused as easily on any of the several other excellent groups demining in Angola and other mine-polluted countries, such as the Halo Trust or Norwegian People's Aid. These, and the numerous agencies working with victims, are not to be overlooked or in any way slighted by omission from these pages.

Because much of Angola was still isolated by land mines at the time of my last visit and because the war has created considerable *confusão*, as Angolans say with a smile, I could not independently verify accounts of battles that were described to me, often years afterward, by former soldiers, refugees, and people who once lived in the affected areas. The details, along with descriptions of who laid the mines, are as exact as I could obtain. Much of what I portray here was a photograph of Angola in the 1990s. The overall picture will change with time – the number of victims worldwide and efforts to improve their lives, the amount of land made safe and the methods of doing it, and perhaps the security situation so crucial to successful mine clearance.

I hope this book will serve to illustrate the scope of the mine problem and the complexity of removing land mines in a country with a long history of conflict. I mainly hope this portrait will show what these indiscriminate and long-lasting weapons do on a daily basis to women, children, and men who had little to do with prosecuting a war and who have little voice in any world forum.

i

"No One Knows
Where the Mines Are Buried"

These days only beetles and termites travel across the old Sangondo battlefield with impunity, and razor-edged dry grass makes the only sound, an undulating whisper in the dawn breeze. The rustling grass and then, as the sun climbs over the massif, the bird-like downward trill of hand-held metal detectors searching the rubble of war. There's a lot of it. Hundreds of men and boys died here, leaving their stories buried in the red clay. Brass cartridge cases and jagged shrapnel from countless thousands of mortar and artillery shells, rusted ration tins and Russian ammunition boxes, steel helmets and belt buckles and truck axles and corrugated iron sheets that once covered bunkers–they carpet the battleground to the horizons and speak in mournful whistles to the metal detectors. Old black basketball sneakers and sun-bleached bone fragments lie mixed with the steel and make no sound at all. Examining the exhibits in this open-air battle museum can take days or months, as much time as the living want to spend here.

Francisco Muiengo keeps sweeping his detector over one spot and getting the same signal. The Ebinger detector, more than $2,000 worth of German technology, tells the young mine-clearance engineer one thing: A large piece of metal is buried here. It says nothing about explosives. Muiengo sets the detector down behind him and picks up a metal probe, a foot-long tool that resembles a kitchen knife-sharpening implement. Turning to his watcher, who sits on his haunches ten meters back and never takes his eyes off his point man, Muiengo gives a nod.

The watcher blows a whistle, signaling other deminers nearby to stop work.

Squatting, Muiengo gently probes the earth at a thirty-degree angle until he feels resistance. Then, using a two-dollar garden trowel and a three-inch paint brush, he fills in the details.

As he scrapes and brushes with the precision of a surgeon, a black plastic disk appears. He knows what he's got. Or at least part of what he's got. Slightly bigger than a quarter, it's the pressure plate of an MAI-75 antipersonnel mine made in Nicolae Ceausescu's Romania and designed to take a man's leg off below the knee. The mine has lain here, undisturbed and deadly, since it was planted five years ago. Muiengo's practiced fingers avoid the plate.

Team supervisor Paulo Generoso, compact and stocky, stands back on his heels and stuffs his hands into the oversized arm holes of his flak jacket. He looks like the hardened army sergeant he once was. His black eyes stay riveted on Muiengo's hands working around the top of the mine. Occasionally, Generoso takes over the steel probe, a master chef giving a critical stir to a delicate dish.

"I think there's maybe something underneath," Generoso says softly. "We'll check it."

They have a good idea what's underneath. The Ebinger suggested a large piece of metal, and the MAI-75 contains only a few small metallic components. More probing reveals the outline of a Russian TM-57 antitank mine, seven kilograms of high explosive TNT inside two kilograms of green steel casing. The picture comes to life like a photograph in a darkroom developing tray.

This combination of lethal devices is known in the mine-clearance trade as a reinforced mine. The MAI-75, nine centimeters across, serves as fuze for the antitank mine, an explosive cherry sitting on top of a larger explosive cake. No one is quite sure why Angolan soldiers used the two together in areas where their attackers were more likely to be on foot than in tanks, except to create a huge explosion, an overkill meant to terrorize survivors by the sheer destructive power of the blast.

They may also have been short of antitank mine fuzes or, more likely, had an abundance of the small and lightweight Romanian mines. Explosive devices of all shapes and sizes from Eastern Europe, Russia, China, the United States, and South Africa were not in short supply in Angola's civil war.

Generoso checks the rest of the deminers, who've been working in parallel meter-wide strips, to make sure they're sitting down. If these mines blow, he and Muiengo will die, but flying shrapnel will miss the others.

Their view takes in nothing of what stood here before the fighting. Above the chest-high grass, a few red-flowering poinsettia bushes give the only hint of Sangondo village. Closer and lower down, trailers of purple morning glories snake through the ruins of what people say used to be the prettiest village in the area, boasting a regional hospital, neat rows of tawny mud brick houses, piped water, and prime farmland that grew maize and mangoes, sweet potatoes and goats and cattle.

In 1991, UNITA guerrillas were pushing from the south and east trying to capture Luena, Mexico Province's capital four kilometers (two-and-a-half miles) away. Government troops put up a stiff defense, and battle lines shifted back and forth, much as French and German lines did in France in 1916 but on a smaller scale. Sangondo's villagers, caught in the middle, fled to Luena, from where they could hear the big guns and mortars pounding their farms. Government soldiers of the Forças Armadas Populares de Libertação de Angola (FAPLA) laid mines, mostly from the Soviet Union and Warsaw Pact countries, in thick belts around Sangondo. The mines did little to stop advancing rebels, who also laid mines to protect their own positions and, eventually, their retreat.

UNITA rebels finally gave up their push and settled in some kilometers back, and remaining FAPLA troops finished leveling whatever the guns had missed. Soldiers looted bricks, windows, doors, roofing tiles, and even the water pipes from homes and hospital, figuring the materials would no longer be needed by the 4,500 former residents now camped in Luena along with tens of thousands of other war-displaced. The village of Sangondo disappeared. The departing armies left behind what wasn't worth stealing, along with thousands of unexploded shells and land mines. Villagers wanting to come home will have to wait for Generoso and his British-trained engineers to clear the mines.

It's a tall order. The Mines Advisory Group, the British charity playing a leading role in demining this province, has been told by former villagers and by the army that thirty-two hectares (that's 320,000 square meters, or seventy-nine acres) around Sangondo are *definitely* mined. But the villagers will not move back until the entire region has been pronounced safe. This means that an adjoining tract of farmland measuring six kilometers by two kilometers (3.7 miles by 1.2 miles), almost thirty-eight times the size of the relatively small area known to be mined, lies fallow.

Surveying – that means determining where the mines are and where they aren't – and then the cleanup operation, by hand and meter by meter, will in all likelihood last longer than it took for FAPLA and UNITA to destroy Sangondo in the first place.

Satisfied that the other engineers have assumed safe positions, Generoso turns back to the immediate problem and nods. Muiengo shifts from a squat to a prone position, his body stretched out on safe ground behind him. He's at eyeball level with the mine, his nose inches from the pressure plate. His fingers move, nothing else. Even the grass has gone quiet. Sweat soaks into his heavy Kevlar vest and drips down the inside of his helmet's plastic visor into the excavation. As he dusts off the mine, two parallel holes appear on either side of the pressure plate. Are the holes blocked with dirt or are they clear? If his hand slips and depresses the pad or if the mine spontaneously detonates, the flak jackets and helmets will save neither man. The combined explosion of the antipersonnel mine and the antitank mine will gouge a crater a meter deep, shred Muiengo from the waist up, and leave little of Generoso other than chips of bone and scraps of fabric.

Holding the mine firmly around its middle in his left hand, Muiengo guides two pieces of stiff steel wire through the holes until they stick out the other side. With the wires in place, the pressure pad can't move. For what seems like the first time in twenty minutes, Muiengo exhales as he unscrews the Bakelite mine body into its two half-spheres. He unscrews the detonator from inside the top half, gingerly in case heat from his fingers sets it off, dumps the chunk of plastic explosive into his hand, and sets aside the components, now safe.

Generoso tells Muiengo to take a break, and twenty-five-year-old Fernando Chendo takes the paint brush. Oddly natty in beach sandals and electric green and purple nylon jogging suit under the flak jacket, Chendo clears the soil back from the antitank mine's steel casing. At a depth of twenty centimeters, years of rain and sun have baked the soil into rock-hard clay, the same clay Sangondo villagers once used to make bricks.

The antitank mine is unfuzed but could be booby-trapped. Antitank mines here are frequently found in stacks or sitting on top of 120-millimeter mortar shells. The whole device is powerful enough to vaporize a man. Often, it was a way of getting rid of excess ordnance; 120s are heavy, and soldiers are not fond of lugging them any farther than necessary. Chendo and Generoso scrape as close to the bottom of the mine as they can, checking for wires leading away from it, then hook a rope noose around the mine and uncoil the rope to its fifty-meter length. "We'll have to flip it," Generoso says. "We don't know what's underneath." Lying protected in the crater of an earlier explosion, two deminers pull hard on the rope. Nothing happens. The mine is stuck fast in the clay. Generoso walks alone back to the mine, digs some more, and refastens the noose. It's still stuck. He digs again. This time a hard pull pops the mine out of its hole and it lands upside down. No explosion. Staying put, the engineers look at their watches. They'll wait two minutes, in case the mine, or another one underneath, was fitted with a time-delay mechanism. One more sweep with the metal detector to be sure, and a smiling Generoso dumps the mine in the pile to be collected at the end of the day. "I'm pleased, the work went well," Generoso says. He's a man of few words, and this is what he does for a living.

This morning's job, removing two of Angola's long-buried land mines, has taken just under an hour.

No one can say with any accuracy how many land mines are scattered across Moxico or any of Angola's seventeen other provinces, and mine-clearance experts get tired of being asked. United Nations and other officials say it's anywhere between nine and fifteen million mines. The top figure is probably too high, but in the end the numbers matter less than the amount of land they pollute. Moxico, whose 223,000 square kilometers (86,100 square miles) account for nearly one-fifth of Angola's land mass, is one of the three most heavily mined provinces in the country, and vast areas must be considered dangerous until surveyed, marked, or cleared. It particularly matters because Moxico, which shares a long border with both Zambia and Zaire (now the Democratic Republic of Congo), is intended as a gateway and staging point for thousands of Angolan refugees returning from the east. In 1997, more than 300,000 Angolan refugees were awaiting repatriation in camps in Zaire, Zambia, Namibia, and Congo.

Luena, the provincial capital, was a main stop on the Benguela Railway, the major Southern African artery that carried freight from the port of Lobito on Angola's Atlantic coast eastward to Zaire and copper ore westward from Zaire and Zambia. Luena also lies at the juncture of the east-west highway and the main road south from the diamond-producing areas in Lunda Sul and Lunda Norte provinces. Straddling these critical routes, Luena was a strategic pivot, and government troops and rebels battled hard for its approaches and airport. Many provincial towns and villages changed hands several times. Luena remained, barely, a government-held island in UNITA territory.

Both sides laid mines defensively to protect military positions, and both practiced what's euphemistically known as "nuisance" or "social" mining, setting out the weapons to terrorize civilians and control their movements. Land mines, or the perception of their presence, are an extraordinarily effective way of canalizing or confining human beings who might seek shelter or help somewhere else.

By the tens of thousands, mines were sprinkled around cities, villages, farms, airports, bridges, power stations, electric pylons, factories, reservoirs, and cemeteries, along rivers and rail lines and under roads and footpaths connecting remote hamlets. Roadside ditches were mined to kill panic-stricken soldiers diving out of trucks just blown up by anti-tank mines. More mines were placed behind and under the twisted truck carcasses to deter rescue and make sure the road stayed closed. A local army brigadier ringed his private farm with mines to deter hungry thieves; his neatly-terraced garden is the greenest in Luena.

In the Luena headquarters of the Mines Advisory Group, dozens of red pins dot a map scaled large enough to show individual buildings and tracks through the bush. By mid-1996 MAG mine specialists, working with information from villagers, farmers, and former soldiers, had identified 183 mined areas in Moxico Province. They also had trained more than 120 Angolan deminers such as Generoso and plotted a long-term clearance operation aimed at returning agricultural land piece by piece to villagers across northern Moxico. Waving a hand over the red pins, MAG senior specialist Dave Turner says, "We think this is just the tip of the iceberg. The final picture will be many times more than this."

Vast areas of this and other provinces are isolated behind UNITA lines or are inaccessible because, as the deminers say over and over, *No one knows where the mines are buried.*

Army manuals in most countries say that minefields should be mapped and marked. In Angola, Cuban troops who supported the Marxist MPLA forces in the 1970s did map some of their minefields, and, to a lesser extent, UNITA rebels did the same. But for the most part, advancing and retreating armies planted mines without recording their location. It's a rare army who thinks about how the land will be used after the war. Trying to establish the size of a minefield can be like asking how long is a piece of string, and finding the mines in Angola is particularly difficult because most of them were laid before 1991. Many of the original mine layers, soldiers who might have been able to say in broad terms where they were, took their secrets to their graves.

Land mines, both antipersonnel and antitank, come in dozens of varieties, shapes, sizes, colors, and degrees of sophistication. In 1996, more than sixty-five varieties had been confirmed or reported in Angola. They were manufactured in nineteen countries, including the United States, Italy, Germany, France, and Sweden. Not one was made in Angola. Around the world, mines are individually laid by hand, mechanically dropped in machine-plowed furrows like potatoes, scattered from helicopters, or fired in bunches from artillery pieces and rockets. Most in Angola were set out the old-fashioned way, by hand.

Antipersonnel mines, which are detonated by a force as slight as the pressure of a child's foot, come in two types: blast and fragmentation. Blast mines cripple or kill by the upward force of the explosion; fragmentation mines spew pieces of hot steel that penetrate and tear.

Francisco Muiengo – this seems to be his week – has spotted the trip wire of a Russian POMZ-2 mine, one of the most common fragmentation mines. Cheap to make and easy to use, the POMZ – or lookalikes made in China, Czechoslovakia, North Korea, and Yugoslavia – have been exported to most recent conflicts. They're all over Angola.

Soldiers distribute the cylindrical mines singly, in rows, or in clusters. The two-kilogram cast-iron cylinder is scored into six rows of ten small squares, much the way a candy bar is scored for convenient bites, and sits on a wooden stake driven into the ground. A trip wire stretches, usually at shin height, through dense grass from the mine either to another mine or to an anchor stake that keeps the wire tight. It kills like this:

When a soldier or civilian – the mine doesn't care which – stumbles into the wire, one kilogram of pressure yanks a retaining pin out of the top of the fuze. With the pin gone, a spring-loaded needle hits a percussion cap, which sets off the detonator. That small blast initiates the main charge, seventy-five grams of TNT, which explodes at a rate of nearly seven thousand meters a second. Expanding gases produced by the ignition shatter the iron casing into small squares of iron that fly at high velocity in a 360-degree pattern, killing anyone within a radius of four meters and wounding people up to twenty meters away. The tumbling, jagged fragments cause horrific wounds and strike terror into survivors who panic or freeze, wondering where the next wire is.

Muiengo approaches the POMZ and places his tools beside him. Termites have eaten away the underground part of the support stake, and the mine has fallen on its side. The trip wire is as taut as a piano wire. Using a pair of garden clippers, Muiengo snips dry grass away from the mine and as far down the wire as he can reach. Satisfied that the wire itself is not booby-trapped, he holds one finger down on the fuze-retaining pin and with the other hand cuts the wire. He wraps the fuze with red electrical tape to secure the pin and finally disarms the mine by pulling the detonator out of the explosive core. The cylinder of TNT gives off a bitter, slightly resiny odor.

How does he feel, having just disarmed a mine that could've killed him? "Happy," he says, picking up the Ebinger and tossing a look that suggests it was a silly question. Taking the POMZ, Generoso flips up his helmet visor and shakes Muiengo's hand. Muiengo looks like he thinks that gesture a bit odd, too.

Francisco Muiengo is twenty years old and has been a deminer for less than a year. He earns three hundred dollars a month, about sixty times the salary of an Angolan policeman. The Mines Advisory Group pays him in U.S. dollars as a hedge against galloping Angolan inflation. The blueprint for the POMZ that Muiengo has just disarmed came from a drawing table in the Soviet Union long before he was born. During

Muiengo's lifetime, Soviet designers modified the mine. The grooves on the cast iron casing weren't deep enough, and the mine was fragmenting into two or three large pieces instead of sixty small ones.

"It wasn't doing enough damage to people," says MAG mine specialist Steve Priestley. Soviet engineers machined the grooves deeper, and the mine became more efficient. (Even this version is now old fashioned. The Model A Ford of fragmentation stake mines was replaced by a Mustang: the state arms company of the former Yugoslavia offers a mine with a greater killing zone than the old Russian mines.)

A whistle blast signals the end of the forty-minute shift, and the Delta Four engineers head for the rest area on the edge of the minefield, trading places with another team. The work, in fields littered with both mines and battle trash, demands intense and unwavering concentration. Land mines tolerate no human mistakes and sometimes no human touch at all. And although dry season days are cool, working in the heavy flak jacket and helmet quickly drains energy.

The rest camp blends easily into the old battlefield. Ammunition boxes and shell fragments lie rusting in the old fighting trenches. The engineers' chairs are heavy artillery shell casings driven upside down into the ground. Rusted steel helmets serve as washbasins, with the homey touch of a white-blooming impatiens in between. Lunch – fish heads and *funge*, the maize and cassava staple – is consumed with little chat. Most of the deminers are former soldiers, and the lives of all have been disrupted by the long war. For many, this is their first formal job.

At fifty, graying and wearing horn-rimmed spectacles, Jonas Romeu is the oldest of the MAG Delta Four team and looks as if he should be wearing a tweed jacket instead of a fragmentation vest. For thirty-three years he taught history, Portuguese, and math to children, adults, and finally to refugees until the war ended his teaching career. His home, the city of Luau up on the Zaire border, has been cut off since 1984 by the fighting and mined roads. He last saw his family in 1991. Romeu misses teaching and hopes eventually to take up his profession again. In the meantime, demining, and the salary it brings, will do.

"To be a teacher was helping Angolans, and to be a deminer is also helping Angolans," he says, with the intonation of a teacher accustomed to making historical connections. "People are fed up with war."

Pascoal Muaco, another teacher whose career was shattered by the war, agrees. But like most of these deminers, he wonders if their work could be undone. "So many times in Angola they've said there will be peace, and then they start the war again."

Francisco Candelei, twenty-two years old and a former soldier, figures that every mine he removes brings him one step closer to his hometown, also Luau, which he hasn't seen for eleven years. "I want to help Angolans to be able to move freely, to farm, to build a new Angola. I want to work hard so no more will lose their legs, to protect the children."

Paulo Generoso, the team supervisor, sees no particular irony in the fact that he spends his days clearing land mines fifteen years after he spent many evenings planting them. One way or another, land mines have had a profound impact on the lives of the deminers or their families. For Generoso, mines have struck particularly close to home.

He never intended to be a soldier, but in 1978, the government made the decision for him. A career as a professional soccer player would have suited him better. Growing up in the farm village of Kavungo, fifty kilometers south of the Zaire border in Moxico Province, Generoso studied math, Portuguese, and drawing, but lived for soccer, playing goalie. Even at thirty-eight he moves lightly on the balls of his feet, and it's easy to imagine his chunky frame stopping shots.

"There was no war," Generoso says. "It was a very good life."

When the war did come, he spent five years fighting not UNITA but Frente de Libertação do Enclave de Cabinda (FLEC) rebels in the northern oil-producing enclave of Cabinda. As an artillery sergeant and then as a mortar platoon leader, he laid land mines, including the two types he's removed this morning. "We went out after sunset and laid defensive mines to protect our positions," he says. "You just take the MAI-75 and screw it together, dig a hole for it, and cover it lightly. But we always worked with a map so we knew in the morning where they were."

For soldiers, land mines were tools of war as normal as their mortars and assault rifles. "We were ordered to lay them, and we carried out the orders," Generoso says with a shrug.

But the young soldiers soon learned that land mines did not distinguish between friend and foe. As they lay in their trenches at night, they would hear the mines exploding. When they crept out to their defensive perimeter at first light, they found the remains of small animals but no dead rebels. "We were afraid of the mines, because so many trails were being blown. There were lots of antipersonnel mines." One friend was killed and two others wounded in mine explosions, and Generoso's company lost four vehicles to antitank mines. This was in a tiny area of the tiny Cabinda district, bordering the Congo and separated from the rest of Angola by a thin strip of Zaire.

By the time Generoso left the army in 1982, large areas of the country were cut off by the fighting and his family was scattered. His father had died of hunger and disease, brothers had been killed in battle. His mother had made it to relative safety in Luena, but his sister was trapped somewhere between government and rebel lines in eastern Mexico. He wouldn't see her again until 1987.

Chisola

Chisola Jorgeta Pezo remembers her brother's passion for soccer, but not that he tended the net. She remembers that they lived in different houses in the same village and remembers that they played together as children and that Paulo was big for his age and tough. Other memories of those years have been locked in a private mental photo album, which she seldom opens.

Chisola Pezo and Paulo Generoso are, by American or European family trees, first cousins, sharing the same maternal grandmother. Chisola's mother, Gilyani Pezo, and Paulo's mother, Sarah Pezo, were sisters. But as far as Chisola and Paulo and everyone who knows them are concerned, they are sister and brother.

In the 1950s and 1960s, Portugal faced spreading rebellion across Angola, which it still ruled as an overseas province. But war had not yet come to Kavungo, a village of perhaps ten houses a day's walk north of the Zambezi River. The village takes its name from the Kavungo River, a slow-moving stream easily forded in places during the dry season. With lucky sailing, a stick dropped in the river in the village would flow south into the Lupatchegi River, down to the Zambezi, and finally sweep over Victoria Falls on the Zambia-Zimbabwe border.

But most of the trade in those days was on foot and by road north to the Zaire border. Chisola says that as a child she and her father would herd goats and cows ninety-five kilometers (fifty-nine miles) north to the crossing at Caianda town and trade the animals for blankets and other goods. Her grandfather, who died before she was born, was the headman of a village upriver – not quite royalty, but sufficient title to elevate the social status of successive generations of children. The bush provided game, the river yielded fish, and the rich land, communally owned, grew rice, corn, beans, sweet potatoes, and cassava. A massive tree provided shade and a meeting place in the village center. When Chisola describes the tree, her eyes shift to a point in the distance and you can almost smell the midday heat beyond the tree's shelter. Life granted the essentials, if not luxury.

"Food and clothing were plentiful," she recalls.

Chisola played soccer, too, sometimes on mixed teams with Paulo, who was four years younger. But mainly she helped her mother gather firewood and work the land, preparing for a life that was chosen for her as it was for most Angolan girls. She remembers playing at being a homemaker, boiling tree leaves in little tin cans. Third in a line of thirteen children, she was the youngest of the girls and learned early from her older sisters how to keep her back straight under balanced loads. Her role did not include school. Chisola says the boys went to school, but that for girls there was no money for books. Paulo says his sister wasn't interested. In any case, she never learned to read or write.

There was little need to mark the calendar. The seasons kept time, recording good harvests and bad, births and deaths and marriages.

The first major upheaval came with the death of her father, Sailundo Kakanda, when she was still a child. Her mother, Gilyani, then married a Zairean, who took the family to what he promised would be greener pastures across the border.

By the mid-1970s, internal strife in Zaire was squeezing civilians hard. Chisola's family was resented by hard-pressed Zaireans, who faced growing competition for space and safety. The family dream dissolved, and Chisola and her family joined a gathering stream of refugees – Zaireans and Angolans – all fleeing west.

In her late twenties and with a year-old daughter on her back, Chisola went home to Kavungo. Portuguese rule was over and Agostinho Neto was Angola's first president. The peace would be short. UNITA guerrillas were on the move across the country, backed by South Africa and the United States. The long nightmare had begun.

Today Chisola can cite with assurance three points in her own life's calendar: she is forty-two years old, the horrors started in 1983, and everything else dates from June 1990.

For most of 1983, FAPLA, the government army, held the key eastern city of Cazombo on the Zambezi River. Then, driving south from bases in Zaire, UNITA attacked Cazombo and Kavungo in November, over-running government defenses. Hundreds of families from dozens of hamlets fled in panic and ran to catch up with retreating FAPLA soldiers.

Babies and cooking pots strapped to their backs, women and children tried to stay out front of UNITA guerrillas. Ragtag rebel bands lived off the land, stealing what they could to eat, and were not known to look after the welfare of civilians, especially from captured towns. The civilian rout was so desperate, Chisola and others say, that some women abandoned their babies in the bush.

Four of Chisola's brothers were fighting with FAPLA, and two of them were killed in battle that year. After months in hiding, Gilyani Pezo's strength slipped away. "She just gave up," Chisola says of her mother. Two of her sons were dead, and she could run no more. Gilyani was captured and murdered by UNITA. Her crime: her sons had been in the wrong army.

For the next five months Chisola and her children survived in the bush on honey, wild fruit, and cassava, never staying in one place for long. Her husband shot a lion and traded the meat and skin for the soldiers' rice rations. But the government troops, nearly as battered and hungry as the civilians, were in no position or mood to look after anyone else: recapturing lost territory took priority.

Government troops retook Kavungo the following year. What they got was a pile of rubble. Kavungo's houses, including Chisola's, had been destroyed, animals and crops stolen by retreating rebels. But Kavungo was home and offered again at least a thin buffer of government soldiers.

Now with three children, her parents dead, and the rest of the family dispersed, she built a grass hut where the old house had stood. Rebuilding in the middle of a war was hard enough. Land mines, laid and forgotten by shifting armies, imprisoned them in the ruins; crop land was beyond safe reach.

The villagers took strength from one another. Chisola's support came from Maria Esther Musa. They were the same age, and, except for Chisola's twelve years in Zaire, they had been inseparable – first as playmates, later as refugees. For the next four years, as fighting swirled around them and spread across Angola, they survived together. And somehow, village life went on. Chisola divorced and remarried, chosen, as she describes it, by Loje Canguya, thirty years her senior. She bore three sons, Loje Capalo, Domingos Kayombo, and José Tomas.

Finding food was life's sole, acute focus. They knew that many of the trails out of Kavungo were being mined at night, but staying put meant a slower death. Just after dawn on Thursday, May 12, 1988, Maria Esther set out with friends down a well-used dusty trail to a patch of cassava, the starchy root crop that provides little nutrition but fills the belly and puts weight on babies. Chisola stayed home, minding the children.

Maria Esther never knew what hit her. Suddenly she was sitting by the side of the trail, staring at the bloody remains of her right leg. Above where her foot had been, the jagged ends of the tibia and fibula protruded from the wound. Villagers laid her flat across the handlebars and seat of a bicycle and pushed her to the hospital a kilometer (six-tenths of a mile) away. She had four children, the youngest a two-year-old girl.

Chisola got to the hospital the next day. "Keep my child," Maria begged her. "I will die now."

"You won't die," Chisola soothed, "you won't die." Two weeks later, Maria was taken to Luena hospital and her right leg was amputated below the knee. Three months afterward, she got her crutches. One was aluminum with a plastic elbow brace and rubber hand grip, the other was a home-made steel crutch with a steel elbow brace. The hand grip on one crutch was two inches lower than the grip on the other. The crutches were not provided by the hospital. Maria bought them from a man who was recovering from a gunshot wound.

"They were expensive," she said.

Saturday, June 2, 1990, dawned crisp and clear across northeastern Moxico Province. At the start of the dry season the mosquitoes were mostly gone, and one seasonal deadly threat—malaria—had diminished. But the war raged on, and civilians who did not actively support UNITA were regarded as supporters of the enemy; there was no such thing as neutrality. It was two years and a month after Maria Esther's accident, and food was scarce. Survival meant taking greater risks every day.

In the cool of the early morning, Chisola and a friend, Zhinga, set out down a well-traveled path to dig cassava in a cleared patch along the river where the villagers had so far been left alone. The path was not known to be mined. Chisola, with Zhinga a few meters behind, made it a kilometer (six-tenths of a mile) out of the village.

Like Maria before her, she neither saw the flash nor heard the explosion.

Based on information about who laid mines where in Angola in 1990 and the description of Chisola's wounds, the device she stepped on was most likely one of these:

- AN EAST GERMAN PPM-2, a small blast mine with an electric fuzing system and a small amount of TNT explosive. East Germany laid these mines in profusion along its border with West Germany.
- A CHINESE TYPE 72-A, one of the cheapest mines on the market and one of the most common antipersonnel mines in the world. The distinctive pale green body contains a tiny amount of metal, which can make it hard for

detectors to locate. More advanced versions of the blast weapon are fitted with anti-handling devices that trigger the mine when tilted a few degrees off level. They've also been found in large numbers in Afghanistan, Cambodia, Iraq, Kuwait, Mozambique, Somalia, Thailand, and Vietnam.

- A ROMANIAN MAI-75, perhaps the most common anti-personnel blast mine in Angola. Chisola's brother Paulo is well-acquainted with the type, having both laid them and dug them up. Not counting the safety pin, which a soldier removes when he buries the mine, the MAI-75 contains thirteen separate pieces: a top and bottom half, threaded to screw together to form the black Bakelite body, a pressure plate, another plastic piece, a rubber weatherproofing gasket, a steel spring, two plastic collars, two hinge pins for the collars, an elastic band, a striker pin and a detonator. Sitting in the bottom half of the mine is a half-inch-thick slice of high explosive, a mixture of TNT and RDX, a powerful military variety with the scientific nickname of "cyclonite." Held in the palm of the hand, the whole mine is about the size of a softball cut in half.

Victims seldom see the mines they step on, so they can seldom describe the type. And the blast and its effects often erase the memory of the event. Most makes of antipersonnel blast mines have slightly different mechanisms but similar consequences. If Chisola stepped on the Romanian mine, here's what happened in the blink of an eye:

The weight of her foot depressed the pressure plate onto the steel spring. As the spring compressed, it stretched the rubber band holding two plastic collars against the striker pin. When the collars popped out of the way, the spring let the pin hit the top of the detonator, which exploded and ignited the block of explosive in the mine body.

The main explosion shattered the Bakelite mine case and created a high-pressure wave that roared upward and blasted her right foot off just above the ankle. The blast wave, moving faster than the speed of sound, continued its upward rush between the layers of tissue and through the bones and compartments of muscle in the lower leg. The wave took with it carbonized fragments of the mine casing, bone chips, stones and dirt, and bits of her leather sandal, hurtling the fragments and whatever bacteria lived on them deep into the wound. The blast wave moved with such force that it stripped soft tissue from the bone and damaged muscle far up the leg. The dead muscles provided the bacteria that had been propelled into the wound with a convenient supply of food. Infection set in rapidly as the bacteria began to multiply. The blast also tore pieces of flesh and muscle off five places on the inside of her left leg and the inside of her left wrist. If you look at the pattern and shape of the scars today, you nearly have a photograph of how her body was positioned at the instant the mine exploded.

Thrown off the path, Chisola blacked out. Back in Kavungo, villagers heard a dull explosion and may have seen a small, black cloud mushrooming into the morning sky. No one had any doubt what it meant. Risking other mines, a neighbor, members of her husband's family, and a soldier rushed down the trail, bundled Chisola onto a blanket stretcher, and carried her to a local military hospital. Without removing the already necrotic tissue below the knee, the surgeon sawed off the tibia and fibula at mid-calf, sutured the blood vessels, and trimmed the flaps of skin, finally tucking and closing them inside the wound to form a stump.

Land mine wounds are messy and complex to treat, even for experienced war surgeons working in sterile operating theaters. Inadequately trained field doctors or technicians in the remote regions of Angola and other mine-affected countries frequently make a difficult problem worse. Chisola's amputation was too low.

In pain so severe that it blurred her vision, Chisola waited. "I thought that I would die, and that if I didn't die I would have only one leg," she recalls. Her husband, Loje, came as soon as he got word. Her four children stayed at home, believing their mother was dead.

"Keep the children, I will now die," she told Loje. She then heard the same words she had spoken to Maria in the same hospital two years before.

"You will not die, you will live," her husband said. "This is normal. It is not a big problem."

Remembering, six years later, the muscles in her face go slack. Five days after the accident, her husband brought the baby to see her. "I hurt very much in my soul," she whispers. "I was breast feeding, and the baby had been five days without milk."

As she lay in the room with two other recent mine victims, all she could think about was the children. Medication eased the pain some, and she slipped in and out of consciousness. The wound was gangrenous and the infection spread through the knee joint into the thigh. The room stank of death.

The three older children were brought to the hospital, and Chisola, terrified they would have a similar accident, ordered them not to stray from the village. Paulina, at nine her eldest, was distraught and tried to commit suicide, her mother says. Chisola wanted to return home to look after them but was too ill. Later that week, a United Nations helicopter transferred her to a bigger hospital in Saurimo, 360 kilometers (224 miles) northwest of Kavungo. It was the first time she had been in another Angolan province.

Surgeons there amputated again, this time removing dead and infected muscle in mid-thigh. The surgery stopped the gangrene and saved her life. She spent the next three months in Saurimo hospital, frightened and consumed with worry about the children. No one except her husband visited. When the fever subsided and she was able to leave her bed, she crawled on the floor. Then, for a month, Loje carried her everywhere, even to the toilet, on his back.

She has only one reflective comment on those days: "If I had had poison, I would have killed myself."

She eventually made it to Luena, where most of her children would join her. But village life was over, as were all traces of her independence. Chisola Jorgeta Pezo was added to a lengthening list of numbers and classified as an Internally Displaced Person, an IDP, as they're called, thus falling outside the help mandate of the United Nations refugee agency. She had become one of an estimated 1.2 million Angolans who were refugees in their own country – and one of every 334 who had lost a limb to a land mine. Angola is now said to have the highest number of amputees per inhabitant in the world. Cambodia, with one in 384 people an amputee, is close behind.

Chisola would not return to Kavungo. Continued fighting and the proliferation of mines had closed every road in Moxico Province.

iii

The Road to Canage

"We're going into a potentially dangerous area this morning, and we need some clear rules."

Dave Turner has his team of deminers and the medic lined up in front of the Mines Advisory Group headquarters one Saturday.

"This vehicle," he says, pointing to a white Land Rover, "will lead."

"We know that somewhere along the road there are mines linked to Claymores for a distance of up to two hundred meters," Turner continues. "So the distance between the vehicles must not be less than three hundred meters from Sacassange onward. There is a radio in each vehicle, and that's how we will communicate.

"If you stop and want to piss, *do not go off the road*. And avoid the potholes if you can."

Turner is briefing the Angolan crew before a reconnaissance mission south of Luena. Lack of reliable information about the roads has kept the deminers from driving far outside the provincial capital since 1994. Turner now has a reason to go.

Most roads in Angola have been mined or are connected to other roads that are mined. This is why nothing moves on the roads of Moxico, and why several million Angolan civilians are marooned wherever they happened to be when the war closed its grip around them.

"Okay? You're happy about what you'll be doing if the front vehicle hits a mine? The responsibility of any of you in the second vehicle is to get anyone alive back to Luena as fast as you can," Turner says. "As fast as you safely can," he adds. "There's no point in *you* becoming a casualty. If I'm the casualty, I'll forego the kiss of life, I'll forego that." It's a small joke, and when it's translated into Portuguese, the deminers muster a chuckle.

"Right, let's go."

Sitting in the passenger seat next to Turner, who is driving the lead vehicle, is the man who has convinced Turner and David Rice, MAG's Mines Awareness Officer, that the trip just might be possible. João Mimoso, thirty-two years old, is a former army infantryman and mechanic and for the past two years has had a civilian career that could be described as either exceptionally courageous or wantonly foolish.

Once a month or so, he has driven, or claims to have driven, seventy-one kilometers (forty-four miles) southeast to a village called Canage to salvage anything usable from the dozens of blown up army trucks that litter the highway. Mimoso, a man of limitless optimism and patience, is planning to build his own truck from scratch with the nuts and bolts and other parts he has collected.

Part of Mimoso's daring comes from the fact that since childhood he has known the road and every trail leading off into the bush. His father, a truck driver, used to take him on trips to Lucusse and on down to Lumbala N'Guimbo when he was a small boy. Later, as an infantryman, he was stationed in the area because of his detailed local knowledge. He says he fought in battles up and down the road at the height of the war.

Mimoso, a natural-born entrepreneur, applied to MAG for a job, figuring he and the deminers were meant for each other. In return for a salary, Mimoso proposed to act as a guide, showing the MAG specialists safe areas and danger spots along what unquestionably has been a heavily mined road.

Turner, who, like his British colleagues, is easily bored when sitting still, has itched for months to push MAG clearance operations out of Luena. The UNHCR has designated cities south and east of Luena as receiving points for refugees. But until the mines are removed from under the roads, and especially from farmland off the roads, returning refugees would face terrible risks and mine casualties would certainly rise, Turner and UN officials say.

Turner had received reports that beyond the village of Sacassange, fifteen kilometers (nine miles) out of Luena, the road is dangerous: antitank mines, many of them booby-trapped, are buried and linked to serial fragmentation mines in the ditches. Another report – and this one is a cause for even greater concern – said that antitank mines in the area have been fitted with light-sensitive anti-handling switches. These devices were hatched in minds most devious: when the top of the mine is uncovered, daylight completes an electrical connection and the mine blows up. They are one of the deminer's biggest nightmares.

In his job interview, Mimoso claimed, rather expansively, to know where a lot of mines were as far as Canage. But he replied that light-sensitive mines, until now unconfirmed in Angola, were news to him.

"If you genuinely have a lot of information about that route, you can be very useful to us," Turner had told him. "We need detailed, accurate information. But if your information is inaccurate and we are speeding along and have a serious accident . . ." Turner left the sentence unfinished and Mimoso got the point. Besides, he would be sitting in the lead vehicle.

Turner took Mimoso on as a mechanic and offered him twenty dollars a week on a trial basis. He also hired him as a guide for this particular mission and told him to show up the next morning at seven. Turner badly wants to open the Lucusse road, which is deep behind rebel lines. Little word has come out of the region for years, and no one knows how many mine accidents have occurred or how desperate the condition of civilians.

But the interview left Turner feeling edgy and wondering. Mimoso had sat half slouched across a corner of Turner's desk and wore a smirk that seldom faded under direct questioning. "He says he served two years as the brigadier's mechanic," Turner mused. "And he left the army in 1984! Christ, I left the army in 1984!"

After a twenty-five-year career in the British Army that took him on active tours in Northern Ireland, Germany, Thailand, Belize, Vanuatu, and Oman, Turner is a fair judge of men under difficult conditions. He also knows a lot about land mines, having helped lay them in Oman and having helped clear them in northern Iraq and Kuwait.

Much of MAG's ability to operate in Moxico Province depends on the cooperation of army brigadier José Rafael and on the brigadier's UNITA counterpart, a colonel named Allelujia. The 1994 Lusaka Protocol, which both parties signed, guaranteed freedom of movement for all Angolans, and freedom of movement means getting rid of land mines. But both the army and the rebels tend to be vague about revealing where their mines are, Turner says. The thinking habits of war have not yet been shelved.

The fact that army troops have not traveled this road for a long time worries Turner.

"The brigadier doesn't go anywhere he doesn't absolutely have to go," Turner says. "But a year ago his second-in-command, a colonel, was showing UNAVEM [the United Nations peacekeeping force] around and blew a foot off [when he stepped on a mine], so that tends to focus the mind." He means that neither the brigadier nor anyone else knows for certain the status of the highway.

The best available information may be less than complete, but Turner has driven mined roads before and decides that if this part of Angola is ever to be reopened for business, the mission is worth the risk. He decides to trust Mimoso.

At 7:15 that morning, Turner, in his standard uniform of white T-shirt, shorts, and British Army boots, is pacing deep tracks in the sand in front of headquarters. The demining team and medic have loaded the Land Rovers, but Mimoso is late. Cold feet? "I'll waste a few more minutes having some words with this fuck," Turner growls. The guide finally shows up, and Turner marches him off for a private chat. When we climb into the Land Rovers just before seven-thirty, Mimoso's wise guy grin is gone.

Heading out of Luena in the lead vehicle through a grove of eucalyptus trees, I realize I have butterflies. I've driven down mined roads before, too, but seventy kilometers (nearly forty-four miles) is a long trip on a road that the army admits *it* avoids. I wonder how much Mimoso does know, and how good a judge Turner is, of when to press on and when to turn back.

Unreasonably, I feel somewhat easier when the dirt track turns to tar macadam. MAG's triangular red warning signs with the skull and crossbones and the Portuguese words for "Danger Mines" stand like sentinels at regular intervals but stop a few kilometers out. Turner keeps asking Mimoso what he knows about the road. "Nothing here," Mimoso grunts.

We're now out of radio range with Luena, in touch only with Rice's Land Rover carrying the minesweepers and the medic, three hundred meters behind. Leaning over Turner's shoulder, I start to ask the dumb question of the day: "Is the speed of the car a factor . . ."

Turner finishes the question for me and answers it. "Can you go faster than a mine explodes? No," he says with a smile.

Passing a stone marker for Kilometer 11, Mimoso volunteers his first detailed information. "There are mines in the fields to the right, near old military positions, but it's clear on the left," he says. Turner radios the data to Rice in the car behind, and Rice notes it on a map.

"No mines around this bridge?" Turner asks as we approach a river crossing.

"No," Mimoso says.

"What about the tracks on either side?"

"No."

Turner's eyes keep scanning, left and right, up and down the road. We're doing about sixty kilometers (thirty-seven miles) an hour.

"I'm looking for a feeling," he says when I ask. "A feeling that things are not quite right . . . and I'm quite happy here, it's been well-traveled . . . but I'm not entirely convinced about his knowledge." Though Mimoso speaks no English and the conversation is going through a translator in the back seat, he's probably figured that his commentary is not thoroughly trusted. Turner never leaves anyone in doubt about his thoughts or intentions. Mimoso's face is a mask.

The land has turned to open scrub. In rainy season, the deep-green sawgrass would be head height. Now a few scrawny trees make the only markers in the landscape.

"There are mines off the track to the right," Mimoso says, nodding to a barely visible trail. "The path is mined, and all the area to the left is mined."

Does he really know this, or is he making it up? He could be making it up to make himself look good. He knows we will not walk down the track to find out.

At Kilometer 25 we wonder if we can get the vehicles across the N'dala River. The bridge was blown years ago, and its replacement is a homemade affair, badly eroded. Mimoso says the approaches are definitely mined. Watching my footsteps, I get out and walk across to guide Turner over with hand signals. The Land Rover's tires are barely on solid ground. An inch the wrong way and the car will flip into the river. Turner makes it, and so does Rice's Land Rover.

Turner is driving slowly now and radios Rice: Avoid the potholes. Turner has that "feeling" and the feeling is catching. Avoiding the potholes means driving around them onto the verge. Many people have died doing exactly that. In a manner far too casual to suit Turner, Mimoso keeps pointing out ridges to the left and right that contain mines. There's no small talk.

We pass the Kilometer 34 marker. Beyond it, we may be the first vehicle to travel here since the 1994 cease fire, other than Mimoso on his foraging missions. There are no villages off to the side and nothing to indicate that the land has ever been used. The deserted road stretches straight and flat to the horizon. Clumps of grass grow out of the potholes. What else is in the holes?

Turner stops to check a bunch of dry grass twisted into a knot. Angolans have been taught to mark the location of mines or unexploded shells with signs like this. Mimoso shakes his head. "This isn't to do with mines," he says. "It's someone's personal marker. Someone hid something here and wanted to be able to find it again." How does he know? We drive on.

Materializing out of the road haze, an apparition comes to life. Three men on two rickety bicycles are heading north. The bicycles are loaded down with sacks of charcoal and live chickens in handmade coops. The men are astounded to see vehicles on the road and a bit nervous about who we are. We are equally astounded to see them. Quite apart from the mines, this is no man's land. Few people have any good reason for being here.

One of the men wears a wide-brimmed blue hat with a badge on it and a logo in English saying, "Statewide Security Systems."

"We're okay, he's a policeman," Turner cracks.

The impromptu conference in the middle of the road a long way from anywhere is productive. Rice peppers the men with questions, seeking any scrap of information about the road ahead and mine accidents in the villages on the way to Lucusse, a hundred kilometers (sixty-two miles) farther south. The trio set off from Lucusse two days ago and have camped on the safe macadam at night.

"The road is okay as far as Canage, but past there it's all mined," one says. And the mines continue all the way from Lucusse south to the UNITA stronghold at Lumbala N'Guimbo. The traveler sums up the road below Canage with a wave of the hand: "You can't move."

"Well, this tallies with what UNITA's been telling us," Turner says as we drive off. "I'm happy that we're okay to Canage."

But are we? Bicycles can easily skirt craters in the road, and even if they drive over an antitank mine, their weight might not detonate it.

The wreckage begins at Kilometer 37. The remains of a truck, ambushed in 1988, according to Mimoso, sticks out of a deep crater. Major battles were fought along this road. Small arms cartridge cases and unexploded mortar shells cover the macadam and the hulks of trucks block the road, grass growing up through the rotten steel.

"How do you *know* there are no mines in these holes?" Turner asks. Mimoso is staring out the window and doesn't answer.

As we drive cautiously around the wrecks, he indicates a long stretch of road.

"Mines on both sides in strips four meters wide," he says nonchalantly. Then an old Cuban minefield on the right that runs a thousand meters into the woods. Rice and Turner punch our position into the hand-held Global Positioning System. The satellite-linked device gives them back an eight-figure grid reference, which they'll later transfer to a map.

"Three people were killed here by a mine in 1994," Mimoso says. Russian POMZ fragmentation mines are strung through the dense grass. It's hard to see anything in the vegetation.

Mimoso points to the wreck of a huge truck in the left-hand ditch and says it's mined. Before Turner can stop him, he walks straight to it and lifts a piece of sheet metal away. The medic sets out his stretcher and bag, and the deminers put on their flak jackets. After a painstaking investigation, the device, a steel cylinder poking out of the ground, turns out to be a part of the truck's shattered engine. "I thought it looked odd, maybe some kind of mine we haven't seen here yet," Turner says.

When we stop to examine another wreck, I go for a walk, feeling confident on the hard surface yet still watching for wires and avoiding the potholes. I spot a 120-millimeter mortar shell half buried in the ditch and wonder if it's connected to others. Then I see something on the edge of the road that no one else has seen and call the others over. The device, lying by itself, is brownish-black, a near-perfect sphere slightly bigger than a golf ball. I wonder if it's a bomblet, one of hundreds of munitions packed into a cluster bomb. I may have discovered something new: air-dropped mines and munitions have not been found here before.

Turner and Mimoso arrive together and to my horror Mimoso quickly picks it up and cracks it open on the pavement. He hands me the pieces, which smell vaguely sweet. It's the dessicated hull of a fruit, a guava or passion fruit. "These are good to eat," Mimoso says with a huge grin, and everyone else gets a good laugh. "Yes, I'm very much interested in the trees and flowers here," I say, considerably embarrassed.

My "find" has broken the tension, and we move on. But we've slowed to a crawl. The macadam looks intact but in my mind is wafer-thin and treacherous. I'm reminded of the technique rebels used in Zimbabwe. Guerrillas would saw an oil drum in half and heat the drum red hot on a wood fire. Using logs as handles, they would put the hot half-drum on the tar road, melting out a perfect circle. Dig out the hole, lay an antitank mine, replace the macadam plug, and coat the join with motor oil. The road would look as it did before.

UNITA guerrillas used variants of the technique here. In one, they burrowed under hard roads from the side, laid a mine, and placed a log vertically on top. The weapon would be deep enough to foil metal detectors, but the pressure of a truck wheel would be transferred through the tarmac and the log to the fuze.

Mimoso decides it's show time and signals Turner to stop. Single file and keeping distance between us, we walk into the woods, Mimoso leading the way. A hundred meters in we stop and follow his index finger. The former soldier has a keen memory as well as sharp eyes: half-buried under leaves and grass lies a Claymore mine that he personally laid when his company maintained a defensive position here in 1984.

"Apart from hamburgers, these are probably America's greatest contribution to the world," Turner says with a grin, as he kneels to examine the mine. High explosive detonating cord connects it to a chain of others down the path.

Originally designed in the United States at the end of the Korean War, the Claymore was widely used in Vietnam. Since then it has been made or copied by numerous countries, including South Africa, Yugoslavia, South Korea, Chile, Russia, and Pakistan.

It kills with extraordinary efficiency and is a favorite ambush weapon for irregular forces around the world: U.S. troops in Vietnam would set them out to protect defensive positions; sometimes Viet Cong guerrillas would creep up to the position at night and turn the mines backward to face the Americans. UNITA got plenty of Claymores from the United States and South Africa. The Angolan army captured plenty from UNITA.

Military experts debate whether the Claymore should be classified as a mine. It was mainly intended as a command-detonated weapon but can be easily fitted with a trip wire. When the mine is detonated, its convex face (the mine is conveniently labeled "Front toward enemy") blasts 700 steel balls in a sixty-degree arc out to fifty meters. The Claymore sometimes comes with a kit of optional tree spikes, allowing it to be deployed at head height. UNITA fighters put antitank mines under roads and linked them to a series of Claymores in the ditches. A truck hitting the mine sets off an instantaneous and devastating chain reaction that can kill or maim dozens of people.

Multiply this path and this mine manyfold and it's easy to see why large tracts of Angola are uninhabited.

The mines may have reduced this patch of forest to a no-go area for most people, but Mimoso has made the problem his ally. Having laid many of the mines along these trails, he's turned the woods into his private game preserve, combining his truck salvage trips with a bit of hunting. His cocky grin has returned.

At Kilometer 54, Mimoso's trickle of information turns into a useful flood. Russian antitank mines, mortar shells, and a host of other explosive devices, many of them linked, lie buried just off the road. They all get plotted on the GPS and marked on maps. But Turner points out that it's still just a partial picture.

"He knows probably little more than his own former positions," Turner says. "I still have vast concerns. This is total memory that's going on here."

The mines Mimoso reveals were laid by FAPLA. Where are UNITA's? Fighting raged at close quarters here for several years, and everyone used mines.

Turner is nonetheless pleased to be breaking new ground. His eyes are smiling and he sounds like a bird watcher who has just tiptoed into the nesting ground of the elusive African Hoopoe.

"This is an interesting area, it's the closest we've come to booby traps on a large scale. It's a worthwhile trip, there's no doubt about it whatever."

The trip was not worthwhile for many before us, and the reminders come every twenty meters or so. The undercarriages of troop carriers hang out of craters, barely recognizable. Few of the trucks' passengers would have survived.

In the middle of the road lies a shredded army boot. The other boot and a bleached skull are several meters away, on the side of the road where the soldier stepped on the mine.

Farther on, the remains of an entire supply convoy, thousands of rusted food tins in the back of one truck.

"The government would take a town, then UNITA would cut the road with mines so supplies couldn't get through," Turner says. "That's how siege situations developed."

The mines ensured that villages like Canage remained under siege.

It has taken four hours to travel seventy-one kilometers (forty-four miles). The astonished villagers say we are the first white people to set foot here since 1972. Some of the children have never seen anyone from outside this village. Mimoso is the only Angolan to have made the trip from the provincial capital for the past two years. His lone forays have given him a bit of status as an explorer. He makes the rounds, magnanimously shaking a few proffered hands, then goes off to examine a blown-up truck.

Canage village has consolidated and moved inland from the river in recent years. Land mines planted by the bridge, the old water pump, and the lumberyard gradually closed the place down.

Five hundred or so people live in circular, grass-roofed mud houses, raising chickens and a few crops. They eat what they grow, and they can't go far to grow it. Disease is rife, treatment and medicines consist of whatever the villagers can concoct from herbs and roots.

The bridge over the Canage River was built by Cuban troops in 1985 after rebels blew the other one. The bridge's four corners are still mined, but villagers bathe and get water there anyway. They harvest oranges and mangoes across the bridge, although they suspect the grove is unsafe.

They ask Turner and Rice to get the word out that they are desperate for food, clothing, and medicine. Mined roads have kept relief agencies away. Until today, Canage has been totally cut off from the outside world.

Turner asks which areas they want cleared first.

"We want all the mines moved. They mean we can't use the land," an official says.

Turner explains MAG's plan for clearing the road from Luena. MAG or another agency will have to carefully move the dozens of wrecks, sweep every inch of the road, clear the mines, and mark the known minefields.

"I'm really chuffed," Turner says later. "It feels good opening this place up. It means Lucusse is possible."

Eventually. The clearance operation from Luena will take weeks or months. And only if the army and UNITA cooperate with each other and with the deminers. Do the people of Canage, isolated for so long, believe the war is over?

"For us to see peace," answers one man in ragged clothes, "we will have to see vehicles going from Luena to Lucusse."

For now, only the charcoal traders on their creaky bicycles will ply the route. From the river bridge south, the road to Lucusse lies cracked and cratered and dangerous.

iv

Mutilados

Angolan airplanes and army trucks shuttling across the country in 1990 carried mainly troops, weapons, and ammunition to hard-pressed military garrisons. Cargo manifests did not include crutches for civilian amputees. A woman in Luena might as well have dreamed of being handed the keys to a Rolls Royce as being given a wheelchair. Land mine victims were not on the priority list of either the government or UNITA, who were busy fighting the war or trying to cobble together a peace.

Chisola crawled and was carried until someone in her family came up with the money and bought her a pair of aluminum half-crutches with plastic elbow braces and green rubber hand grips.

She won't look you in the eye when she describes how she learned to walk again sometime after her thirty-sixth birthday.

"It was very difficult. I fell a lot and I often cried," she says, her eyes focusing somewhere beneath the floor.

"I was angry . . . I used to walk very well."

By late that year UNITA had consolidated its gains in eastern and southern provinces and was determined to take Luena and its airport. Chisola and thousands of other civilians who were pushed west by the fighting took shelter wherever they could – in Chisola's case, in what used to be Luena's beer brewery. She had been in the provincial capital a week.

She awoke one night to the sound of UNITA heavy guns pounding the city and the airport. As she lay terrified in the dark, she thought once again that she was about to die.

The bursting shells missed the building. But shrapnel from one sliced through a water basin inches from her head.

The jagged hot splinter also smashed one of her aluminum crutches. "I thought I was very unlucky," she says. "These were the legs that were helping me and now they also are broken. How can I walk now?"

Luena had neither a machine shop nor any organization that supplied the needs of land mine victims. Local craftsmen in the middle of war scavenged their materials from abandoned buildings or trash heaps. Amputees bought what was available. Chisola's replacement crutch, originally made for someone else, was a length of steel pipe. Welded onto the shank was a half circle of steel for the elbow brace. The hand grip, also steel, was two and three-quarter inches lower than the grip on her original remaining crutch. Her mismatched crutches, like Maria Esther's, looked and functioned more like medieval instruments of torture than aids for the handicapped. But she was no longer crawling.

Throughout UNITA's forty-five-day bombardment and siege in 1991 and through three more years of fighting, she lived with other refugees in the brewery until city officials finally evicted them. They were not given a reason, just told to move. Mine victims were treated no differently than other civilians, which meant they were left to fend for themselves.

Along a broad, tree-lined boulevard two kilometers (just over a mile) from the roofless and empty beer factory, half a dozen ocher-painted buildings with red tile roofs and Portuguese archways still inspire admiration from local people who can remember what the city used to be. In 1996, Luena's abandoned railway station stood as the frozen metaphor of a broken country. The last train from the coast is said to have pulled into the station in 1980, and the last train for Zaire left in 1985.

Although war damage in Luena was slight, a few faded signs are about the only reminders of the pottery factory, bakeries, hotels, restaurants, coffee processing plant, and lumber mill of a once-vibrant city nicely snugged in Angola's rice belt. One man thought he even remembered a small factory that produced beeswax for export.

The railway station actually was not abandoned, it just changed function and became home for Chisola and 2,508 other war-displaced Angolans. Camped in the once-grand buildings and ruined boxcars rusted to the tracks, they know how many they are, not because they've been included in a government census but because they've counted themselves. Remnants of village political structure survive in the camps, and officials, themselves refugees, keep track of lives going nowhere.

The provincial bus station is a refugee camp, too, as are several of Luena's schools. In one multistory school, its pink walls smoke-stained from cook fires and empty window frames strung with laundry, teachers conduct desultory classes in the refugee chaos. The teachers receive no salary but cling to their profession, having no other productive way to pass the days.

Although Luena's seventeen shelters for the displaced are equally grim, the symbolic crown of misery rests at the Museum of the Revolution. The museum, built on the city's outskirts to glorify Marxist Angola's triumphs over UNITA, offers visitors a portrait of revolution and war far more graphic than the government ever intended. The only remaining outdoor displays are a rusted UNITA armored personnel carrier, a captured artillery piece, and the shot-up silver fuselage of a South African bomber. Children play in the APC, angling the cannon barrel up and down at imaginary invaders. The carrier's crew cab doubles as a community trash bin. Several families live in the remaining rear half of the bomber, hanging their washing on a line strung from the tail.

There are no exhibits inside the museum. A gaunt man in a white sport shirt emerges with a clipboard from the main hall's sooty windowless interior, runs a pencil to the bottom, and matter-of-factly announces, as though he had been expecting the question, that 2,112 displaced people, most of them from Luau and Cazombo, live in the museum. All have been here for two years or more. One elderly man says he's not sure but thinks he arrived in 1991 or 1992.

All 2,112 are wholly dependent on emergency rations of corn, beans, rice, and oil donated by the United States and the European Union. One man has spread half-fermented corn to dry in the sun to make the potent local home brew. His clothes hang from his bony frame in tatters and he's rolling drunk at ten in the morning. Women pound corn for meal and wash dishes in plastic tubs.

Relief agencies say they can't be certain but figure that as many as 80,000 internal refugees are stuck in Luena, doubling the city's prewar population.

At the railway station, Chisola sits on a sack of rocks under a eucalyptus tree, trying to warm her malarial chills in the morning sun. The rocks look like those lying between the railroad tracks.

"We collected them in case builders want to buy them," she shrugs. A handful of international agencies are fixing up rented houses and offices in Luena, and the refugees thought they saw a commercial opportunity. Piles of steel rail ties were carried off to make animal fences around town. The rusty fences are still up, but most of the animals were eaten long ago.

Walking toward the station at sunrise, it's possible to imagine mornings in Chisola's hometown of Kavungo before the war. Crying babies and the rhythmic thump of wooden pestles in wooden mortars would have begun the days there, too. Smoke from the charcoal braziers rises straight into the crowns of the eucalyptus trees, carrying the smell of boiling corn meal as it would have in Kavungo.

Inside, the conjured similes end abruptly. For privacy, families have partitioned the old ticket hall into makeshift rooms with bits of sticks and plastic sacking. A soot-streaked election poster of President dos Santos, smiling in a suit and tie, papers over the gaps on one of the partitions. Residents say it's the closest dos Santos or any government official has been to the station since the trains stopped running, and the photo was not put up as a tribute. (Officials of the ruling Marxist MPLA party did visit some of the displaced people before the 1992 elections but didn't ask for their vote. "They *told* us how to vote and we followed," one woman said. "If we refused, there would've been a problem.")

The concrete floors, walls, bits of sacking, and even the air are varying shades of black, gray, or brown and are saturated with smells of wood smoke, unwashed bodies, and human waste. The women keep the place as clean as they can, but small children with diarrhea often can't make it to the outside pit toilets. Racking coughs echo off the station walls. During rainy season, water pours through the shell holes in the roof, and even in the dry months Chisola and her neighbors wrap in blankets to keep warm.

The only decoration on the bare walls is an oil portrait of a bearded soldier in government uniform, with the shoulder boards of a FAPLA officer. The portrait bears a striking resemblance to UNITA rebel leader Jonas Savimbi, the enemy commander. The subject of the painting, older now and minus the beard, hasn't noticed the likeness before and finds it an amusing joke. Apart from the crucifix on a chain around his neck, and a few pots and pans, the painting is about all the former soldier owns.

Privately owned trucks pass daily along the boulevard to fill water drums for anyone who can come up with the equivalent of a dollar. The water, parasite-laden, comes from the river and is drunk untreated.

Food is meager and the living conditions desperate, but the province's mined and impassable roads have produced an odd consequence: Luena's air is unpolluted and sweet and the untrafficked nighttime streets are quiet.

Quiet except for bursts of unexplained gunfire and the hymns. Malnutrition, tuberculosis, and especially malaria take a heavy toll in the camps and *bairros*. Mosquito-carried malarial parasites kill quickly, mostly children, but adults, too. Several times a week *a cappella* hymns echo through the darkness, nightlong wakes that precede morning funerals. Even speeding army trucks slow and pull off the road for a baby's casket strapped to the back of a bicycle pushed by the minister with the congregational procession behind.

Since the accident, Chisola has buried two of her infant children this way. She can recall neither the dates nor what killed them. What matters is feeding the youngest children who survived – Maria Manusha, now three, and Loje and José, aged eight and five. Manusha and José were born in the camps.

Her face looks chiseled from black rock. High cheekbones under a high forehead, broad nose, and long-lashed almond-shaped eyes with laugh lines at the corners give her a somehow regal look. Her eyes hint at something, mischief possibly, waiting to break out, and she smiles frequently. With friends and when warmed up, she leans into a conversation like a boat into a headwind, hands punctuating her discourse in rapid-fire Luwale.

She stands a wiry five feet, two inches, and when leaning on the crutches looks precariously unbalanced, her body alignment permanently distorted by the uneven support. But over the years she has compensated for the three-inch difference in the hand grips and perfected a gait that is fluid and swift. Using one crutch like a hockey stick, she deftly knocks a tin can out of her path without missing a beat. Today the lower crutch is on the right side, and her right hip and shoulder dip three inches with each step. Occasionally, to distribute the discomfort, she switches the lower and heavier steel crutch to the other side. To free her hands for other chores, she perches like a bird by hooking the stump of her right leg over one of the hand grips.

At the bottom of the station platform, the two women adjust their crutches and Chisola sets a rolled rag cushion on her head. Maria Esther, leaning on one crutch and tucking the other underneath her arm, helps Chisola lift a fifty-kilogram (110-pound) sack of ground corn onto her head-cushion. With the sack slightly offset, Chisola rewraps her *chitengi*, wriggles to fine-balance the weight, and the two amputees, one of them under a load that might make a man twice her size blanch, set off for Luena's main market. The day before, she hauled the corn to a mill across from the station and paid a few dollars to have it ground into meal. She'll spend the next several days selling the meal in the market for a profit that is tiny but still a profit. What she earns is enough for basic foodstuffs for the children and for water and cooking charcoal. Meat of any sort is usually unaffordable. Any money left over is invested in more corn. The corn, donated by the United States and distributed by the UN's World Food Program, was not meant to be resold, but in Angola market conditions make the rules.

The weight, whether it's a sack of grain on her head or the baby on her back, forcibly tilts her pelvis off level, which in turn puts abnormal pressure on her lumbar vertebrae and sciatic nerve, shooting bolts of pain down one side and through the hip. In addition, fragments of the land mine may still be lodged in her right thigh, which swells and throbs six years after the amputation. The steel brace has worn thick callouses on the backs of both arms below the elbow. She does not mention these things unless asked.

Her left sandal hits the pavement fifty-two times a minute and her even pace, roughly equal to that of a physically fit American on a country stroll, gets her to the market in eighteen minutes, with a couple of brief stops to exchange greetings with other women.

An outside observer can experience a strange and almost embarrassing phenomenon when walking with Chisola. The crutches and the fifty kilos (110 pounds) of meal occasionally seem to vanish: She could have two legs and be chatting with friends on a street in London.

Many Angolans seem to experience the same thing. On the way to the market, a soldier approaching from the opposite direction sees someone behind Chisola he wants to talk to and stops directly in front of her. Chisola pulls up short and waits until he finally steps slightly to one side. The soldier gives no indication he has seen her.

Land mine victims, *mutilados* in Portuguese, become nearly invisible to a public preoccupied with their own problems.

"There are too many of them," says Ulrich Tietze, the program director of Medico International, the German humanitarian charity setting up a rehabilitation program in Luena. "It's like car accident victims in

Germany or the United States." He means that Angolans with both legs just don't notice the amputees. Tietze cites the example of his Angolan driver who, on seeing *mutilados* in the road, leans on the horn. (Angolans are, however, egalitarian in their driving habits: they blast the horn liberally at all pedestrians.)

Based on preliminary estimates, Medico International figures there are fourteen hundred mine amputees in Luena and its sprawling *bairros*, including many who've come from other parts of Moxico Province. Medico estimates that 46 percent of the amputees are women and children. These are victims on the government side of the confrontation line; no one can hazard a guess how many there are behind UNITA lines, where relief agencies were just beginning to venture.

According to today's best estimate, there may be thirty thousand amputees nationally. Some sources double the figure.

Sitting in the market, Chisola agrees that amputees are either ignored or shunned. "When people see me, they think I'm coming to beg something to eat. They say, 'We're not worried about you, we're not the ones who injured you.'"

A local Angolan official who started a weekly feeding program for mine victims remarked to an international relief worker that the amputees were so pushy that he had grown to dread the day.

"They expect special treatment!" he complained.

The phenomenon has been observed in other heavily mined countries like Cambodia; amputees are seen as a nuisance and as less than whole beings.

Chisola knows the feeling.

"I think sometimes I'm not a person. I'm an animal." She's looking at the ground when she says it, but spits the words out.

The *mutilados* and the *deslocados*, the war-displaced, are also soft targets, especially for the police, who, like many civil servants, have not been paid for months and have, as the saying goes, "empty bellies and full AKs" (the ubiquitous Soviet-made AK-47 assault rifle).

Amputees say they are frequently beaten and robbed. On one occasion, members of the elite and well-armed Rapid Reaction Police, nick-named the Ninjas, burst into the market and began firing automatic weapons into the air. Chisola and the other traders dove for cover. When it was all over, her stock of corn meal was gone. Another time, according to an international charity, soldiers threw a grenade into a market packed with civilians, killing four people, including a child, and wounding eleven.

When Chisola considered poisoning herself after the accident, she knew what lay ahead and how she would be treated with a double handi-cap: *a woman amputee.*

The loss of a limb accords no special status for age or gender, and women feel uniquely vulnerable. Walking through a busy *bairro* one Sunday, Chisola suddenly broke into a lope and hid behind a hedge until a man in a yellow T-shirt, who had been walking behind her, was a safe distance away. The same man had molested her on at least one occasion before, she said.

Angolan men, accustomed to acting like they run things whether they do or not, seem to have a particularly hard time adjusting to the loss of a limb.

The only hostility I encountered from amputees in Angola, and it happened only twice, came from men, a civilian and a former soldier. One, who had a brown plastic prosthesis from mid-thigh, drunkenly insisted that I examine and photograph his false leg. I wasn't sure if he was proud or ashamed of it.

Another, who as a civilian stands much less chance than a soldier of ever getting an artificial leg, was drunk enough that it was easier for him to lean against a wall than to navigate on crutches. He waved his stump at me, raging and spluttering unintelligibly, also demanding a photo-graph. Chisola, who is respectfully known around the railway station as "mother," intervened with a lecture about rudeness, and the man sul-lenly staggered off.

Medico International's Tietze tells of interviewing a group of mine victims, seven men and three women, at the station one day. One of the men talked about his particular humiliation.

"I'm like a woman!" he shouted. "Everyone can tell me, 'Sit down and don't get up again.' I'm like a wife!"

The women amputees, Tietze recalls, were laughing. They knew what the man was talking about and weren't particularly sympathetic.

Tietze also questioned a group of sixty amputees and asked two basic questions: "Since you stepped on a mine, have you been visited by either a village headman or a government official?" All sixty said they had received no such visit. The second question was "Who, if anyone, is helping you with your everyday activities?" All gave the same answer: family members.

A visit to Luena's Central Hospital shows on any given day how critical family support can be to a mine victim. For example, one Tuesday toward the end of May, twenty-one-year-old Tomas Jonas decided to accompany his uncle to work at Luena airport. Jonas was unemployed, and the walk provided a diversion. The airport is surrounded by minefields, and the dangers are well-known. Jonas and his uncle took the main paved road. On the way home Jonas decided to take a shortcut through an overgrown field. The mine took off his right leg at the knee, mangled the other one, and threw him five meters off the path. "I thought I was dreaming," he says. When the waves of pain hit, he knew he was not. A week later he lies on the bare mattress of his hospital bed, covered in a green blanket and looking at the blood seeping through the bandage. Too weak to prop himself up on his elbows for more than a minute, he asks a visitor to give a message to anyone who will listen: "I want the people who sell mines to stop selling them to Angola. They are very dangerous weapons." Jonas's wife, Jodiki, sits on the edge of the mattress. She has brought an orange, water, and a small box of food, which sit on her husband's bedside table. Barring unstoppable gangrene, Jonas will likely survive.

Sitting up on another bed, steel springs jutting from the dirty mattress, João Adolfo stares with empty eyes out an open window at the hospital's only scenic attraction, a tree in the courtyard with flame-orange flowers in full bloom. Two months earlier Adolfo, who is forty years old, left Alto Campo for the bush, looking for firewood to sell. The mine took off one leg and blasted his body with shrapnel. "I thought I was dead, and I started crying," he recalls in a voice barely audible. MAG deminers working nearby heard the explosion and got him out of the minefield and to a hospital. Eight weeks after his leg was amputated, his skin hangs in folds from a skeletal frame. He is too weak to walk, even if he had crutches. He has neither a wife nor children to bring him food and depends on small handouts from other patients. The hospital, like most in Angola, does not serve meals. Adolfo's survival is not assured.

Hospital director Dr. Manuel Nzinga chain-smokes cigarettes down to the filter and looks a bit guilty when he does it. "I know, it's very danger-ous . . . but we have big problems here," he says with a shrug.

Nzinga, an orthopedic surgeon and internist, has been Central's chief doctor for two years. He and three other doctors staff the 350-bed hospital. Two of the four are Vietnamese, holdovers from the days when Communist countries exchanged such courtesies. The Vietnamese, it's said, are paid between three and nine dollars a month, sometimes noth-ing at all, receive no subsidy from home, and are as hungry as their pa-tients.

Nzinga says the hospital has treated more than 300 mine casualties in the past two years. He figures he has personally performed at least fifty amputations.

For a time, mine casualties poured into the hospital at the rate of ten a week. The numbers have decreased to about one a month.

"But the point you have to realize," he says, pulling in a lungful of smoke, "is that many [of the casualties] didn't make it to hospital. No one knows how many died."

(The unknown numbers haunt everyone. The International Com-mittee of the Red Cross says there is reason to believe anecdotal evidence that for every victim admitted to a hospital in Angola, Mozambique, Somalia, and Afghanistan, another dies without treatment.)

Nzinga, black hair flecked with white, tucks his gold-framed glasses into the pocket of his short-sleeved sport shirt and walks briskly as he gives a visitor a tour of the hospital. Down dank and unlit corridors, their walls and ceilings cracked from a 1991 artillery bombardment, Nzinga has to find someone with a key to open the operating room. Keeping it locked seems an eccentric precaution. Both X-ray machines are broken, one of them for the past six years. The anesthesia machine is broken, and only four of the bulbs in the nine-bulb overhead lamp work. By way of demonstration, Nzinga pumps a foot pedal to raise and lower the twenty-year-old, Portuguese-made operating table. There's nothing else in the room except an empty cabinet and two discarded hypodermic needles lying on a steel table.

Anesthesia is administered by spinal injection. In the absence of a respirator, patients are left to breathe on their own during surgery.

Small quantities of antibiotics are occasionally available, Nzinga says, but in most cases, whether or not a patient gets medicine depends on the foraging instincts and financial ability of the patient's relatives.

"The doctor tells the family what type of medicine they should look for at the market and then they go buy it." Sometimes the relatives can't find or afford it, and some patients have died as a result, Nzinga admits.

When considering the array of problems, Nzinga spreads his hands wide. "It's not only Angola. All over the world the conditions are like in Angola. Before, we had all kinds of medicine here, but when the war started, everything started falling apart."

All of this he accepts with the calm of a war zone surgeon. But when he looks at the amputees, his eyes harden.

"People who make the mines *know* that mines kill, and they send them to Angola to kill. I wish those people would stop making mines.

"Land mines are not a gift. They are death. The war has destroyed the Angolan people. We do not want to live in this way."

Listening to the conversation, surgical nurse Maria Filomena's eyes are blazing, but she is reluctant to speak her mind to a foreigner until Nzinga prods her. When she does speak, her words are knives.

"People who make land mines should put them in their own countries."

Whatever is in their hearts, Filomena and Nzinga are telling only part of the story. Later, Filomena unintentionally opens a page on it.

These days malaria kills more Angolans than land mines do. In midmorning, Filomena and another nurse are wheeling the body of a middle-aged woman who has just died of malaria from a hospital ward to the mortuary in another building. The woman's daughter, holding the hand of her own infant son, wails in grief as the nurses pull the stretcher across the sandy courtyard.

Seeing me, Filomena stops and straightens up. "Hey, we're hungry, give us something to eat," she says bitterly.

Soldiers, police officers, office workers, and all their families are hungry unless someone is well-connected to high-ranking party officials. Nurses like Filomena are no exception.

Dr. Catherine Delbrassine, a Belgian physician with Médecins sans Frontières, does not smoke, and it's a good thing. If she had the habit, she would chain-smoke the way Nzinga does. Instead, she uses drastic body language and chops the air with her hands when she talks. Delbrassine and a Belgian nurse run an emergency feeding program for several hundred malnourished babies across from the hospital morgue, and Delbrassine, like the other MSF volunteers, is overstressed and fed up.

"Everything is completely disorganized," she says. Surgical and nursing skills are far below acceptable levels, and most Angolan hospital staff show little interest in patient welfare, she and many other foreigners say.

Nurses in Luena go unpaid for four to six months at a time and, in Delbrassine's words, "are under great pressure."

As a result, she and other aid workers say, medicines supplied to the hospital by international donors are stolen within a day of arrival and sold in local markets. Frustrated at seeing its urgently needed supplies winding up in market stalls, M S F began padlocking medicines in a secure room and doling them out to hospital staff on a quota basis. "We say, 'There's your meds for the day, that's it, that's all you're going to get,'" says one foreign volunteer.

Medico International's Tietze is equally dismissive of the oft-stated good intentions of hospital personnel.

"They have two new ambulance cars, Nissan Patrols, I think, but they're used as taxis for the doctors," he says. "Only one old one is used for the patients, and there's no equipment inside. This [attitude] makes it very difficult for us to help."

Tietze, a physicist and medical engineer by profession, says hospital administrators make frequent requests for equipment donations, but he's not entirely sure why they ask.

"They want to have the finest equipment, but they just want to *have* it. Nobody is really honest here."

Most Angolans know from long experience how the system works, whom it benefits and whom it does not. Land mine victims know they're at the bottom of the social heap and regard complaining as a time-wasting luxury.

"I'm not thinking anything," Chisola says flatly. "I'm just living."

When it's pointed out, rather unnecessarily, that carrying fifty kilos (110 pounds) of corn would be considered by most societies an unreasonable burden for a slightly built woman with one leg, Chisola looks as though she has misheard.

"I have to eat. What else can I do?"

V

"Mines Are Not My Problem"

When the dull thud of an explosion rolls over the city at one o'clock on a Friday afternoon, no one braces or dives for cover. It's a punctuation mark in the day, like a factory whistle: scattered cheers break out in the market and a round of applause on the streets.

Mines Advisory Group engineers have just destroyed their weekly collection of mines, rockets, and grenades, and the thought flits through more than a few civilian minds: That's one less for us.

Peeling off their flak jackets as the open truck rattles through town on the way back to headquarters, the young Angolan deminers, high-spirited on payday, exchange banter and toss remarks at the girls on the side of the road. The girls flash smiles back.

And when the British mine specialists go by in their Land Rovers, children give chase with the thumbs-up sign and yell, "Amigo, hey, amigo!" If they catch the foreigners on foot, they're likely to shyly add, "*Dinheiro, por favor* [a little money, please]." The foreigners return the smiles and thumbs-up signs, in a ritual repeated dozens of times a day.

As MAG and other mine-clearance groups inch their way through the rings of minefields strangling roads and cities, they are gradually helping give Angolans what the MPLA and UNITA promised by signing 1994 Lusaka Protocol: freedom of movement.

To the children and the *deslocados*, the foreign deminers are the closest to heroes they've ever had.

Angolan authorities sometimes seem less enthusiastic about the foreigners. Instances of creatively erected obstacles provide a regular supply of teatime chat.

One British deminer tells this story:

In 1995, the year after the government gave MAG the green light to begin lifting mines in Moxico, the British specialists hired local builders and began converting an old school into a mine-clearance training camp. A year later the local education minister began hinting that rent payments might be appropriate. When MAG balked at the change with a reminder that they were a nonprofit charity, the education minister decided the deminers could not use the school at all and would have to leave.

"But you understand we are clearing mines and saving the lives of children here," one of the deminers protested.

Unmoved, the education minister replied: "Mines are not my problem."

The deminer said he knew the minister had children of his own. Didn't he care that this charity was working to make the land safer for his children? The well-dressed minister coolly repeated his earlier comment: "Mines are not my problem."

"What he meant," said the deminer, still steaming, "was that *his* children will never be anywhere *close* to a minefield." MAG dug in its heels, the government backed down, and work went ahead.

The MAG payroll in 1996 pumped more than $10,000 a week into a local economy bled dry by more than twenty years of war. When MAG put the word out that it would start a training course for thirty new engineers, more than three hundred local men applied. A deminer's seventy-five-dollar weekly paycheck, a staggering salary in local terms, usually helps support a large or extended family. It also attracts jealousy. Angolan engineers say the police frequently shake them down.

Mine clearance was well underway by mid-1996. Humanitarian and commercial companies from Britain, Germany, the United States, Norway, South Africa, and the United Nations had established themselves in several provinces. To coordinate operations, the UN's Central Mines

Action Office (CMAO), a branch of the Department of Humanitarian Affairs, set up offices in a Luanda high-rise where intermittent power failures frequently leave elevator cars stuck between floors. To speak to someone in another office, it's often quicker to walk up a few flights of stairs than to get through on the telephone.

CMAO, with successes behind it in Cambodia and other countries, aims to link road and farmland mine clearance in order to pave the way for the safe travel of internally displaced Angolans and refugees.

The aim is also to teach managerial and technical skills so that the Angolan government can take over all mine clearance operations in four or five years. Toward that end, the government created the Instuto Nacional de Remoção de Obstáculos e Engenhos Explosivos (the National Institute for the Removal of Explosive Obstacles, which, for the sake of convenience, is always referred to by its Portuguese acronym, INAROE).

INAROE, which is headed by two high-ranking former military officers – one from the army, the other from UNITA – has its office down the hall from CMAO. The two bodies meet daily to talk over strategy, tactics, and problems. Disagreements are a frequent feature of the discussions.

The MPLA and UNITA, in theory bound together in a government of national unity, have formally pledged themselves to ridding the country of land mines.

But both sides vividly remember broken cease-fires and promises of the past and find it difficult to put aside their distrust and weapons of war. The occasional ambivalence toward mine clearance is also closely entwined with the war-wrecked economy and endemic official corruption.

It all leaves reality a bit blurred and the mine clearers feeling somewhat like Sisyphus in Hades, endlessly rolling the same rock up the hill.

To finance the war after Moscow shut off the tap, the government sold oil futures, spending lavishly on weapons without leaving enough for the salaries of police, teachers, and health workers. Disgruntled civil servants, desperate to feed their families, staged rolling strikes. (UNITA served civilians under its control little better; while smuggling diamonds to stock its own arsenals, the rebels, according to people who traveled widely behind their lines, provided no health care for civilians and routinely stole crops. As one UN official put it, "There's no philanthropy in UNITA.")

The International Monetary Fund, seeing no government progress on economic reform, suspended a monitoring program that could have led to loans. International aid donors lectured both sides and warned that they were losing patience.

Ordinary Angolans did not need to be told that the situation was grim. Pay hikes, when they were given, were instantly devoured by inflation that reportedly reached 3,000 percent at the end of 1995. Devaluation, accomplished by knocking several zeros off the ever-larger denominations of the national currency, the *kwanza*, only compounded consumers' frustration. A near-worthless *kwanza*, coupled with steadily rising prices, meant that when Angolans went shopping they left home with plastic carrier bags full of money.

For a foreigner, the easiest way to comprehend the wildly fluctuating currency and its effects was to measure it. That June, I tried.

Two million *kwanzas*, at the time, was worth ten U.S. dollars. In a stack of 100,000-*kwanza* notes, then the largest available denomination, that sum was one inch thick. In 50,000-*kwanza* notes, the most common, the equivalent of ten dollars was two inches thick. Filling a shopping trolley with groceries could easily consume several stacks of mixed-denomination bills.

Paying for the groceries can be a fascinating but time-consuming experience. Since it would take an unacceptably long time to count tens of millions of *kwanzas* by hand, cashiers use bank-style machines that flip through bundles of notes in a minute or so. Watching the bills whiz through the machine and pile up on the counter top provides a lesson in the economy of war while standing in the queue.

It was still getting out of hand, and the government was rumored to be planning to issue a new half-million *kwanza* note.

Eddie Banks, then the UN demining chief, and his wife Pat got a freeze-frame portrait of the *kwanza's* dizzying daily plunge. When they informed a Luanda hotel clerk one afternoon that they would be checking out the next day, the clerk got out his calculator.

"If you pay your bill this afternoon, it'll come to one hundred ninety million *kwanzas*," he said. "But if you wait until tomorrow morning to pay, it'll be one-hundred-ninety-four-and-a-half million *kwanzas*."

For foreigners who are paid in dollars, it's an inconvenience at worst. For Angolans paid in their own currency, it means that foodstuffs and other consumer goods daily recede from reach.

"When you *do* get paid," said one long-serving government worker, holding his thumb and index finger a half inch apart, "it's just for today and tomorrow."

Earlier, Eddie and Pat Banks experienced firsthand the extreme measures that inflation can provoke in civil servants: they were robbed at gunpoint by uniformed policemen outside their hotel.

The imploding official economy only fueled the black market and slowed whatever production there was. "With hyperinflation, people earning *kwanzas* would get their paychecks and then be absent from work for three days because they'd immediately buy things to trade on the street," one Western diplomat said.

Theft and corruption, which has reached dazzling proportions, has a major impact on all foreign organizations operating in Angola. Humanitarian deminers and other volunteers are not exempt. "It's the most difficult country I have ever worked in," says the veteran director of one European relief agency.

Because of the high cost of airfreight from Europe or the United States, most foreign aid missions ship their trucks, spare parts, and supplies by sea. Luanda's port may well be the leakiest in Africa.

Theft from the docks, with government taxes and duties heaped on top, can bring expensive delays.

Some agencies report that trucks shipped by sea sit in Luanda port for as long as ten months, while their administrators wade through a seemingly endless registration process and haggle with local bureaucrats. When MAG finally got a truck released from the port after weeks of bureaucratic postponements, the truck's jack, toolbox, fire extinguisher, spare parts kit, and even the gas cap had been stolen and the oil drained from the crankcase. The truck then sat in front of MAG's Luanda office for several more weeks awaiting license plates to be issued.

One humanitarian worker tells of watching a procession of just-released trucks leaving the port through a human robbery gauntlet lining the road. "One guy was even disconnecting a truck's battery as it drove along," he said in amazement.

Foreign charity workers frequently say their work is deliberately impeded. "Everyone wants a bribe to get a stamp on a piece of paper to get things done," one says.

Some government officials are known to be unhappy that foreign humanitarian groups like MAG regularly bring in large sums of cash and pay local workers directly: it creates pockets of prosperity beyond their control. The government announced that it would soon require MAG's Angolan engineers to pay 2 percent of their salaries and MAG itself to chip in another 18 percent of those same salaries, all of which would go into a government fund for social insurance in case any of the deminers got ill or hurt.

Past social insurance funds have all vanished into an official void, foreign observers say.

One aid worker dismissed the proposed tax as a thinly disguised way of taking cream from what the government sees as a free-roaming cash cow.

"What this country needs is to pull together as a team," the worker said. "The people have had enough of war, and all the government thinks about is lining their own pockets."

A co-worker, who has spent more than two years in Angola, agreed. "They're going to milk the NGOs for whatever they can," he said.

Government officials in Moxico Province declined to be interviewed about the complaints.

Land denial caused by mines is as economically crippling on a large scale as the physical injuries are on an individual level. For instance, while much of the land around the hamlet of Canhengue may be safe enough to farm, just ten kilometers (six miles) away in Luena the World Food Program is providing emergency food for eight thousand former Canhengue residents too frightened of the mines to return home and rebuild their lives. Relief workers also worry that after years in the dreary camps, many people once self-sufficient on their own land have grown dependent on a long-term international welfare plan.

Even worse, others charge that Moxico Province officials may have deliberately exaggerated the figure of eight thousand dependents. As long as the cargo planes keep landing, local government officials have plenty of supplies that can generate profits in various ways.

As perverse as it sounds, this story is commonly told in Angola. The governor of Malange Province, which lies to the northwest of Moxico, is widely reputed to be a master of business acumen and survival under wartime conditions. His pink stucco home would not look out of place in Beverly Hills. A senior UN official confirmed this tale: After the rebel siege of Malange was lifted (it lasted longer than the siege of Luena) and local people began tilling whatever fields were safe, the governor ordered soldiers to destroy the new crops. As long as civilians remained unable to feed themselves, the UN would maintain the flow of donated food, part of which would be handed over to soldiers, on whom the governor depends for personal security. A similar scenario occurred in Uíge Province in the north, the UN official said.

(The alleged crop destruction in Malange triggered another event in an enfeebling chain reaction: UNITA guerrillas, nervous at seeing government troops roaming around the fields, reportedly laid new minefields to ensure that whatever the army was doing, it wouldn't encroach on civilian territory they controlled.)

Some foreign diplomats say that the Angolan government, whatever its deficiencies and despite occasionally frosty relations with international charities, does appreciate what the NGOs are trying to do. Although the government is constrained by a legacy of xenophobia and blinkered by the tenets of Marxist central planning, it does give the mine-clearance firms a "fairly free hand," the UN official said.

"Everyone in the government understands the importance of opening up the roads and the infrastructure and the impact that would have on the economy," said one Western diplomat. "I think the government wants to get rid of the mines. But [the problem is that] neither side trusts each other."

Another facet of the problem is that, despite a stated commitment to removing mines, the government in Luanda cannot always control its army commanders in the field or its civilian provincial governors who have carved out cozy home turfs. And the mines may even serve to keep civilians under control, some people say.

"Mines are not only a weapon, they're part of politics," says Ulrich Tietze of Medico International. "The government is not unhappy that people can't move in some places. My impression is that the government lives quite well with the mines."

Peter Simpkin, who retired in 1996 as director of the UN's Humanitarian Assistance Coordination Unit (UCAH), agreed that the welfare of Angolan civilians is still a low priority. He believes that until the government revises its attitudes toward civilians, little will improve.

"Angolans have no rights whatever," Simpkin said a few days before leaving to return to England. "Until there is free circulation of people, we'll have a state of sub-subsistence economy with severe shortages, no market, high inflation fueled by shortages of products, and a rapid deterioration of the infrastructure."

Simpkin, who, like many international workers, has an abiding fondness for the Angolan people, was departing with a gloomy assessment of what land mines and the long civil war have done to the country.

"I would say that much of the infrastructure is unrepairable after twenty years, and it applies to both sides. Nobody fills in a hole. No one actually gets out of a truck to throw a few rocks into the hole, they just drive around it, and eventually the road disappears."

And until the government finally sheds the last of its old Marxist skin, Simpkin says, the holes will just get deeper.

"The only hope for Angola is private enterprise. They should lift restrictions on visas and work permits and allow people to lease land. I think it'll take years to rebuild the government. It's so weak."

Conceding that economic turmoil was spinning out of control, President dos Santos shuffled his cabinet in early June 1996, naming Fernando José França van-Dúnem Prime Minister (it was van-Dúnem's second appointed term as Prime Minister: he served from July 1991 until after the October 1992 elections).

At his inauguration, van-Dúnem made it sound as if his government had just been jolted from a long slumber: "Our priority is effectively to give solutions to the problems of hunger, health, education, and misery," the *Jornal de Angola* quoted him as saying.

Dos Santos urged cabinet ministries "to pay salaries which have been delayed for some time." But the president hastened to add that an improved standard of living wasn't all that mattered.

"Priority has to be given to defense and internal order as well as [to] social assistance," the newspaper reported him saying.

Use of the antipersonnel mine may top the list of military habits hardest to give up. Asking insurgent armies such as the mujahideen in Afghanistan or the Khmer Rouge in Cambodia to destroy stockpiles of mines is a bit like asking Iraq's Saddam Hussein in 1990 to hand over his supplies of chemical weapons.

The little weapon has been called "the perfect soldier": always alert and ready to kill, never in need of rest or food, and unaffected by the weather. For irregular forces who travel mostly on foot with little armor, the antipersonnel mine offers good value for the money. It's cheap, lightweight, easy to transport and deploy, and inflicts terror and chaos as well as injury.

"It's their best weapon," Turner says.

The U.S. Army has praised mines as a "force multiplier." It means that small or thinly spread forces using them can achieve battlefield advantages that far exceed their numbers or logistical capability.

It's a heady power not lost on individual soldiers, rogue units, or even civilians in conflicts around the globe.

In Bosnia and Croatia, civilians forced out of their homes by fighting sometimes placed antipersonnel mines and booby traps around the house and garden before fleeing, hoping to deter looters and occupiers.

In Angola, a soldier in an engineering battalion stationed outside Luena got drunk one night after a dispute with some of his officers. In a fit of pique, the soldier laid mines in the road, closing it for hours until the UN and then MAG specialists were called in and negotiated the mines' removal. No one was hurt.

In Sangondo, the army brigadier gave MAG permission to start clearing mines from the old battlefield, but the operation bogged down when a local police commander, defying the army, threatened to lay even more mines if clearance began. This, too, required negotiation, and a sizable part of the minefield remained untouched.

Both the army and UNITA privately make it clear that in many areas they rely on the mines, and intend for now to keep some, no matter what the peace agreement says about freedom of movement.

A cautious and hard-eyed man who has seen much combat in his twenty-one years of military service, army Brigadier Rafael reveals little to an interviewer. But he does give a glimpse of the occasionally schizoid thinking of many soldiers on the subject of mines.

"We in the military are allowed to have mines," Rafael told me, somewhat defensively. Then he added: "Civilian Angolans want the mines to be removed. We would like our country to be free of mines." He went on to blame the bulk of the mine problem on UNITA.

Luena's airport, which is of considerable strategic importance to Rafael's command, offers an example of the unsettled military situation and the continuing impact of mines on civilians. ⁄

Should the airport ever fall to UNITA in a bout of renewed fighting,

Rafael would lose his only adequate supply line into the province. The airfield is surrounded by thick minefields on three sides; army engineers laid blast mines and chains of fragmentation mines around a nearby school and only meters from long-established homes. The school was later abandoned, but Alto Campo Sul residents had nowhere else to go and still live with the danger. Turner refers to the airport as "the biggest killer in the area." As far as the army is concerned, it's the villagers' bad luck that they happen to live next to the airport.

Lauleta Iemba says she doesn't know how old she is but has lived in Alto Campo Sul for at least fifty years.

The villagers grow sweet potatoes, corn, and bananas in closely packed little patches between the houses and mango trees. "We don't use the land. We are afraid of the mines," she says.

Over the past three years Iemba remembers seven mine accidents — three people maimed and four killed. One of the dead, according to Turner, was a police officer who stepped on a massive reinforced mine: "It vaporized him. There was nothing left."

The army has told the deminers that with the exception of a few fields, the entire airport perimeter is strictly off limits. To illustrate how extensive the minefields are, Turner describes how he evacuated one casualty.

"We heard the bang and drove there as quickly as we could. Three or four kilometers was as close as we could get with a vehicle. We took a stretcher and a medic and we ran along this track for ages, and kept asking people where he was, and they kept saying 'farther in.' When we found him, he was on the edge of the minefield; some of his friends had got him almost out but didn't know what to do next. He lost a foot above the ankle. He was lucky we were there."

MAG's Steve Priestley says the army has added to the minefield in recent months, although there's been no indication that UNITA is planning an attack. The army denies it and says it has laid no mines since 1993.

The people of Alto Campo Sul would be delighted to see the land cleared. "So we can move freely again," the elderly woman says.

The army's touchiness is nothing new. Throughout the war, fighters made it known to the outside world that they welcomed humanitarian assistance only when it was convenient to the battle schedule.

During the siege of the cities, the UN's World Food Program had to negotiate with both sides for landing permission for every flight carrying emergency food supplies to civilians. Flights were often grounded or shot at, and operations halted for weeks at a time.

It's the same story trying to clean up after the fighting. Turner, Priestley, and Rice spend a good deal of their time trying to persuade the former combatants to let them lift the mines.

The soldiers seem unsure why foreigners want to *do* this.

"Neither side can understand why NGOs would want to come in and sort out somebody else's problems," Turner says. "Especially when it means putting *ourselves* in dangerous positions!"

As the senior British mine specialist, Turner commands respect in the officer ranks on both sides. Square-jawed and crew-cut, he still comfortably wears the habits and manners acquired of long military service. With the Angolans, he's blunt and unflinching and gets MAG's humanitarian pitch across by talking ex-soldier to serving soldier. He, Priestley, and Rice continually fly MAG's credo of strict neutrality and emphasize that they are unconcerned with the military situation, beyond how it affects safety.

"I made it clear to the brigadier that I would tell him nothing about the other side, and I'm telling UNITA the same thing. And neither side seems to have any trouble accepting that."

MAG believes that many civilian casualties could be reduced if the armies would agree to consistently mark all known minefields. In the event of renewed fighting, security would not be compromised, Turner and other military experts say.

"I was able to explain [to the brigadier], as a soldier, that there was no reason for him *not* to mark his minefields," Turner says. "If it came down to the crunch, he could take the signs down in nothing flat. It was a line between giving him advice and telling him what he was doing wasn't necessary."

(Ironically, and sometimes tragically, civilians often defeat this effort to protect them. The markers, a white skull and crossbones on a red plastic triangle fixed to an iron rod, are driven into the ground at regular intervals around minefields. Villagers and farmers, figuring that they've been warned, steal them for building materials; it doesn't help newcomers. MAG now sinks the bars two feet deep in a concrete base.)

The army is receptive to mine clearance, but the doors are not yet wide open. Rice says the brigadier and provincial officials complain that MAG is concentrating on removing mines only from the government side.

Rice responds: "Your minefields are killing local people, and we *are* trying to get into UNITA areas, and we *are* lifting UNITA mines."

Rafael does have a point, however. UNITA is even more reluctant than he is to give up its weapons.

At Sacassange, southeast of Luena, UNITA is believed to be operating a clandestine diamond mine – their own cash cow. When villagers asked MAG to help get rid of some of the land mines, Turner approached a rebel commander for permission to clear part of the area. He got a blunt reply: "If we see you there, we'll shoot you."

vi

Turner, Priestley, and Rice

The Russian air crew weren't quite home and dry, but the mission was half accomplished, and white-knuckle supply flights for the UN's World Food Program often got measured like that during the war. Seconds after the last bag of corn had been thrown out of the hold, the Antonov-12 was off the apron and roaring full throttle down the shell-pocked runway. Luena airport in 1993 was the heart of the besieged army garrison deep inside rebel-held territory, and UNITA feared that any aircraft might be carrying enemy weapons or troops. It was not a place to loiter.

Minutes later, as the cargo plane climbed on a northwest heading back to Luanda, UNITA gunners opened fire from the jungle below. Their aim was accurate. The pilot turned the damaged and smoking airplane around but couldn't maintain altitude and crashed just outside of Luena. The crew, six Russians and one Angolan, figured they were lucky to have survived. What they didn't know was that they had crash-landed in the middle of an unmarked minefield. Shaken, they climbed out of the wreck and began to walk away, hoping they were not still in rebel gunsights. They didn't get far. The exploding land mine killed the flight engineer and wounded several others. Three years later, the tail of the airplane sticks out of the brown scrub across the valley from the abandoned village of Canhengue. The hillsides are still mined, and no one goes near the wreckage.

Land mines were not kind to humanitarian workers around the world in 1993. The International Committee of the Red Cross lists these incidents between January and November:

- SIX SENEGALESE RED CROSS workers killed when their vehicle hit a mine
- TWO MOZAMBICANS KILLED and three others wounded by a mine
- FIVE PEOPLE, THREE of them ICRC workers, killed by a mine in Somalia
- THREE DEMINERS, ONE French and two Pakistanis, killed by mines in Kuwait
- ONE LOCAL RED CROSS worker killed and three others seriously wounded when a Belgian truck was blown up by a mine in Rwanda

Relief workers know the hazards of working in active war zones. They are often unprepared for the dangers of the peace that follows.

"You look for trip wires or stakes, you look for mine fragments or the remains of animals . . . and if you see the remains of humans, it means you're too late and you're already in the minefield." Standing behind a display of antipersonnel and antitank mines meant to impress, Dave Turner is briefing a detachment of newly arrived Brazilian troops attached to the United Nations Angola Verification Mission (UNAVEM III), who may face some of the same risks as Angolan civilians.

"If one of your men has an accident, stay calm. When you have a friend in front of you screaming in agony, it's an instinct to rush to help him. It's a bad mistake. If you are stuck in a minefield and don't know the way out, the only way is to prod," Turner continues, demonstrating the technique.

"You keep at it, a centimeter at a time. It is a very, very long process. You have to clear enough for your own body. Then you carry the casualty out of the minefield . . . *before you give him first aid!*"

As he hammers away on the theme that mines respect neither civilians nor peacekeepers, Turner wonders if the survival message is getting through. Only a few of the camouflage-clad Brazilians seem to be listening. The rest seem more interested in taking souvenir snapshots and photograph each other, in designer sunglasses, chests thrust forward, against the backdrop of the land mines. Two of the soldiers have heavily bandaged feet; the wounds were acquired on a soccer field. Turner hopes the peacekeepers will finish their Angolan duty tour with injuries no more serious.

A few months before the Brazilian peacekeepers arrived in Angola in 1996, American troops were spreading out across the snow-covered fields of Bosnia with NATO's Implementation Force (IFOR). In February, an American soldier died when a land mine he picked up exploded in his face. The soldier would have been thoroughly briefed on the hazards of mines in Bosnia. For whatever reason, he broke the rules.

Turner, like most soldiers since the Second World War, was well-trained in mine warfare. In 1976, Britain was assisting the Sultan of Oman, who was fighting rebels backed by the neighboring People's Democratic Republic of Yemen, and Turner was seconded from the British Army as an adviser to the Omani Army's Corps of Engineers. As a combat engineer, he specialized in both mining and mine clearance. Omani troops under Turner's command laid mines along a dry watercourse, seeing to it that the minefield was mapped and, usually, fenced or marked.

"We never thought about it," Turner says, looking back over what was a routine military tactic. "We were asked to lay mines on top of a *wadi* . . . it never occurred to us that someday, somebody who had nothing to do with the war was going to get hurt." In one part of Oman, British Royal Engineers had laid forty-five kilometers (twenty-eight miles) of British-made antipersonnel mines across the desert to block the rebels' camel routes from the Omani coast – the so-called "Hornbeam Line." When the war ended, Turner helped clear most of that minefield.

Turner retired from the army on a full pension in 1984. The pension wasn't quite enough to live on and he wasn't ready for retirement anyway. He worked for a security company and managed a series of parking lots and a shopping mall, commuting daily into London. "It was very stifling," he says.

When the Gulf War began, Turner knew where he belonged: the vast quantity of unexploded shells and land mines strewn across Kuwait's oil fields, desert, and beaches would have to be removed afterward. He landed a job with Royal Ordnance, the privatized successor to Britain's state arms company, and spent the next year helping clean up shells and rockets (but not land mines) from the battlefield.

Ordnance-disposal experts from several countries paid heavily for working in the desert littered with more ammunition than anyone had ever seen in one place. So many U.S. Rockeye antitank cluster bombs had failed to explode that one expert described them sticking out of the sand "like a field of tulips."

As a Royal Ordnance disposal team began loading the contents of an Iraqi ammunition dump onto a truck one day, something – an unstable shell or fuze – was mishandled and the whole load blew up, killing five and injuring many more.

"There were bits of bodies everywhere," Turner says. "There was one man still alive with his eyes wide open, and we couldn't figure out why at first. Then we saw that he was looking at the bottom half of a colleague. It was quite a strange sight. We arranged for something to block his view, and then we spent the rest of the afternoon picking up pieces of meat."

While disposing of the leftover ordnance, Turner and other former soldiers also were paying close attention to the biggest scourge of the brief war: the mines. Some of the minefields in Kuwait had been marked or fenced and had been laid in patterns. Many more had been created randomly. But the desert was flat, the sand easy to probe, and the whole country would fit inside the borders of Massachusetts. Most important, the war was decisively over and Kuwait and the allies were committed to getting rid of the mines. Money was not a problem for the government of Kuwait; commercial companies poured into the Gulf state. Many months and $750 million later, when just under two million mines had been found and destroyed, the UN says, the operation was declared successfully completed. Some experts, however, say many of the mines remain.

Complete or not, removing mines from Kuwait was cleaning peas from a dinner plate compared to dealing with the menace elsewhere. Stories of appalling civilian casualties had begun coming out of Afghanistan, Cambodia, and Somalia. Human rights groups and relief agencies were publicizing the stories and demanding that antipersonnel mines be outlawed. The Mines Advisory Group, a small British charity started by another army veteran and his wife, was conducting land mine surveys in Afghanistan. Its founder and director, Rae McGrath, was a blunt and unrelenting campaigner and the international media had jumped on the story. Dave Turner grabbed the phone.

"It was more than the money," he says, "the job was tailored to my experience."

His first assignment with MAG was Kurdistan in Northern Iraq, where mines laid by Saddam Hussein's troops were taking an awful toll on civilians. In the rocky mountains of Iraq, Turner's second career was born.

"We had cleared some land, and a family returned right on our heels when it was safe and began rebuilding their old house. And for the first time, I realized the amount of satisfaction you could get from returning people to their land – satisfaction to be gained in a big way."

The satisfaction, seldom voiced, is the main reason Turner and many others risk crippling injury far from home to disable some of the world's deadliest weapons.

When Steve Priestley returns to Luena after three weeks' home leave, he drops his bags on the living room floor and settles down with a mug of tea, scratching his new tattoo, a multicolored Grim Reaper on his bicep with the logo "Live to Ride." (The tattoo reflects his love of high-performance motorcycles rather than an attitude about what he does for a living.) Small talk about the holiday and family in England can wait. He's more interested in what Turner has to say. "It's amazing how much has changed in three weeks, I can't believe how much Delta Three [one of the MAG teams] has done," he says, when he hears which areas have been cleared.

Turner nods in agreement. "There'll be a lot of progress this month, too—it's nice and cool."

After eight years as a bomb disposal expert in Britain's Territorial Army, the equivalent of the U.S. Reserves, Priestley also logged a year in Kuwait before being hired by MAG.

"It's addictive, challenging, and exciting work, working with explosives generally," he says, echoing the sentiments of many bomb-disposal experts. And it's more than a job.

"Having children myself and seeing the situation in a country where children are being blown up twenty years after the mines were laid . . . if I were in that situation, I would hope someone would come along and help me."

Without bothering to unpack, Priestley drains his tea and changes into shorts and a red T-shirt with a large skull and crossbones on the front and back, the wearable version of MAG's warning signs. Adjusting a two-way radio, he heads for the minefields to check on the teams.

The MAG house in Luena will not make it into *Better Homes and Gardens*: no pictures on the walls, the furniture a garish collection of wobbly plastic lawn chairs and blue vinyl couches, one with hazardous protruding springs. The residents scarcely notice, nor do their occasional visitors, other relief workers whose own living rooms aren't much fancier. Turner, Priestley, and Rice shun the few social get-togethers organized by other international agencies and are regarded by some as standoffish.

"They don't *drink*, you know," other relief workers sometimes say.

The no-booze rule is self-imposed. MAG does not allow its Angolan deminers to drink because no one can afford to be in a minefield under a fog of alcohol. A deminer who shows up for work smelling of drink is fired on the spot. MAG figures the standards they apply to their employees should apply to themselves as well. Visitors find it hard to believe that army veterans who dig up land mines for a living don't party hard. Priestley, Rice, and Turner prize the remarks as compliments. "Even our bosses in England think we're weird because we don't drink," Turner says, with a bit of pride. Safety aside, digging up land mines in a helmet and fragmentation vest twelve degrees south of the Equator leaves little enthusiasm for partying.

They're out the door at six-thirty in the morning, back for lunch, and the workday ends when the sun goes down. After dinner and the nightly radio call to the MAG administrator in Luanda, entertainment, if they can stay awake for it, is likely to be a video (electricity comes from a generator). The choice is usually the abrasive comedy of Scottish comedian Billy Connolly, an action movie, or a documentary about the Gulf War or – what else? – mine clearance. One favorite, frequently shown to visitors, is a documentary about another British company that for a time had a commercial contract in Somalia. The video shows teams of Somali deminers working shoulder to shoulder, instead of safely spaced, while their British supervisors look on. If a mine exploded, it would wound or kill several instead of one. "They look like they're bloody digging in a garden," Turner says disparagingly about their probing technique.

The video, which Turner shows to illustrate how demining should not be done, gives him a measure of satisfaction because of MAG's own safety standards. It also casts a worrisome shadow. The commercial venture in Somalia failed because of bungled finances and the complexities of operating in a country with ongoing political problems.

Successful humanitarian mine clearance, apart from the physical rigors, could be likened to a long lever resting on a tiny and precisely placed fulcrum: money. Nonprofit agencies like MAG depend entirely on donated, UN- or government-allocated funds rather than commercial contracts, and nothing about humanitarian demining comes cheap. The fulcrum must be continually oiled.

Picture one of MAG's Angolan deminers. Francisco Muiengo is wearing a flak jacket and ballistic helmet that cost about $600. His metal detector costs another $2,500. The reconditioned surplus truck that takes him to the minefield every morning costs in excess of $8,000. His salary is $300 a month. Envision him standing in a line with more than 100 other deminers with the same equipment and that in one month they have cleared an area the size of two soccer fields in a province the size of Minnesota. Now imagine clearing land mines by hand from all the fields and woods of Minnesota, then multiply that several times until it becomes the size of Angola. None of this includes the cost of radios, satellite telephone, fax machines, four-wheel-drive vehicles and fuel, air and sea cargo, housing rent, or the salaries and war-zone insurance for the deminers.

The small picture looks like this: MAG's operation in Moxico Province, including a planned expansion to the south and east of Luena, was budgeted at approximately $3 million for fiscal year 1997.

Some of the costs, in both money and time, are hard to figure in advance.

Priestley, who trains new deminers, found that the long war had disrupted or outright cancelled education for a whole generation of young men. He has to teach many potential engineers from scratch how to read a ruler and do basic math so that they can safely perform critical tasks, such as measuring detonating cord or calculating the weight of demolition charges.

Although the deminers don't intend to, they wind up physically rebuilding a part of whichever war-battered country they work in, and at times the difficulties can come down to something as ordinary as a bag of cement. If you live in Minneapolis and want a few bags to make a backyard patio, you can drive to the local building supply store, spend less than fifty dollars, and be back home in under an hour. In Eastern Angola if you need cement to build a training center, the job can turn into a long-distance shopping expedition costing many hundreds of dollars and several weeks. The cement must be bought in Luanda, booked and loaded on a UN cargo flight, and flown 800 kilometers (500 miles) to Luena. The UN's World Food Program, reeling under the costs of its own emergency supply operations, charges charities more than $400 a metric ton for air-shipped cargo. If you're lucky, the cement will not be stolen from either Luanda or Luena airports.

Simple items become exotic imports. When David Rice hired carpenters to build tables and chairs for the camp's classroom and replace windows and doors in the public mine-awareness center, he learned that getting supplies is a recurring problem. Screws and nails, glass, paint, and glue have not been available in Luena for many years. Rice finally found a box of a hundred wood screws in Luanda and paid nineteen dollars for it. He also shelled out sixty dollars for five liters of white gloss paint.

Food is equally expensive. Grocery stores in Luena are shuttered and empty. Local open-air markets offer only fish, oranges or pineapples, onions and carrots, and a few herbs, all at London prices.

"We're about out of soggies," Turner notes one morning at breakfast. Soggies (British Army slang for *cereal*), coffee, milk and sugar, cheese for lunch and stew for dinner, bottled gas to cook the dinner, and soap to do the dishes all come by air from the capital and are much appreciated when they arrive.

When the supply lines from Luanda or from England falter, the complaints in Luena may be sprinkled army-fashion with rude words but are half-hearted and fleeting. It may seem a corny concept, but Priestley, Rice, and Turner would rather work than gripe.

Rice, a thirty-year-old former school teacher from London, spent his first week in Luena mapping the *bairros* and the centers for the displaced. With the aid of a Global Positioning System, maps, and countless meetings and interviews, he is plotting a larger map: where the mines are and where accidents have occurred over the years.

"People do know about mines, of course," Rice says. "The difficulty is assessing the risks for them, finding out who goes where and why, and how they're living their lives. It's sitting down with people and talking about issues *related* to mines – gathering food and firewood and so on – and getting them involved in intelligence gathering. Then we're getting people together with military commanders and pooling intelligence."

But war leaves long memories. Angolans in the polarized and fearful countryside have learned to their pain that talking can be as dangerous as the minefields. They have been told that areas were strategically mined (whether they were or not) and that land mines must be treated as military secrets. Civilians suspected of revealing such secrets or even harboring sympathies for the other side were tortured or executed during the war and today are still reluctant to reveal what they know.

Rice is frequently struck by the enormity of the problem and by a stubborn political reality: mines are still being used to control the civilian population. South of the N'Dala River, where UNITA allegedly guards its diamond diggings and threatened to shoot MAG engineers, rebels use land mines as what Rice calls "an isolating factor."

"The road into the village is mined, and so you have two villages of about eight hundred people that are totally isolated. They're getting desperate, and they've even begun clearing overgrown bushes off the roads themselves. . . . you have other little villages of a few hundred people – off the road and off the tracks."

As he talks, his eyes keep straying to a large-scale wall map. Blue pins mark the known mined areas, pink ones the land mine incidents since 1995. There are a lot of both.

The eeriest thing about the map is its emptiness: Even when the map was published, in 1988, the war had been on for a long time, and across the grids whole villages with their clusters of houses are marked "abandoned" or "destroyed." In between the clusters are great swatches of green where there are no pins at all, savannah and jungle crisscrossed by networks of rivers and foot trails. Who lives in these remote places? Who walks the narrow trails?

"One of the biggest things that worries me is accessibility. You just don't know what's going on there."

If you look at the map long enough, telescoping down onto the miles of paths that connect the words "abandoned" and "destroyed," you can see it happening: Columns of sweat-soaked men weaving silently through the grass, rifles and grenade launchers on their shoulders, mortar shells and land mines in their backpacks. Villagers in twos and threes, babies on their backs and bundles on their heads, scattering in panic. How many stepped on mines and survived? How many bled to death in the bush?

Rice worries about those empty spots – the rich bottom land and the deserted villages along the rivers – and about the hundreds of thousands of war-displaced and refugees crammed into the railway station and other camps in Luena and across the borders in Zambia and Zaire. If they start pouring into eastern Moxico anytime soon, he'll be sticking more pink pins in the map.

He wants to head east.

vii

Under Siege

The afternoon he returned to Luena, a normally garrulous American demining surveyor had to search for words to describe conditions in the eastern rebel enclave of Cazombo.

"It is right out of the Stone Age," he said, shaking his head.

Food was so scarce, he said, that UN peacekeeping troops, low on supplies, were driving around the airport at night running down rabbits to eat.

The thousand or so civilians in town, lacking the means to hunt rabbits, were dependent on corn, beans, and vegetable oil flown in by the World Food Program, and UNITA soldiers were helping themselves to about half of that. "The soldiers are from age sixteen up, and they are very strong compared to the civilians," he added.

The UN survey team of which he was a part didn't get far out of Cazombo, a single-street town, or what used to be a town, with a dozen *bairros* spread around a UNITA military garrison at the airport. The UN team suffers the same travel limitations as civilians, and a reconnaissance convoy made it thirty-eight kilometers (twenty-four miles) south before turning back to lessen the chance of hitting a mine or getting ambushed in the dark. The mission told them what they largely knew: UNITA controlled both the land and the civilian population, and all roads into Cazombo, except a few from the Zambia border, were blocked by mines. Surrounding farmland was also a no-go area. This data would be logged on UN maps to plan future operations. The UN team, which included an INAROE liaison officer from Luanda, explained to UNITA that Cazombo had been designated a gathering point for thousands of returning refugees, and fields and living space would have to be made safe. (In 1995, more than five thousand refugees did come home, dangerously increasing the demands on scarce crop land and housing.)

Sixty kilometers (thirty-seven miles) north of Cazombo, Chisola's old home village of Kavungo lay beyond reach, a forgotten speck in what amounted to a minefield thousands of kilometers in circumference. Roads to it are mined, bridges are down.

"We wanted to get up there, but we couldn't – there was no way. We heard that some local traders were getting in every couple of months by back roads, but that's all we heard," the surveyor said.

For the UN team and the deminers, villages like Kavungo are still question marks on their headquarters wall maps. This was the first hint in more than four years of any human activity there.

As the UN moved into Cazombo district, MAG was pushing east from Luena.

Caked in red dust, their sleeping bags soaked with spilled diesel fuel, Turner and Rice had just returned from an exploratory mission to Luau. Before the war, Luau, nineteen kilometers (twelve miles) from the Zaire border, was a bustling city and the last eastbound stop in Angola on the Benguela Railway. Getting to Luau these days is a long, bone-grinding journey on deeply rutted sandy roads that cannot be said to be safe. One main road has not been used since the Portuguese left in 1974.

Today, for nearly eleven thousand children, women, and men in Luau, life is worse than in Cazombo, worse than in Luena, maybe worse than anywhere. All traces of civilization have vanished.

UN emergency food flights have not yet begun. There are no shops in Luau and nothing to buy. Money does not exist, neither *kwanzas* nor dollars, because it has no value and no use. If outsiders run out of food and try to buy fruit, they can't pay for it: villagers take soap and salt in barter. When people in the *bairros* see the few outsiders who've made it this far, they ask for clothing.

There is no electricity; the town has a generator but no diesel fuel to run it. Surgical amputations on mine victims are performed without anesthetic in Luau hospital. The only medicines are small quantities trucked in by Médecins sans Frontières; they don't last long.

Casualty figures, those that are reported, are consistent with minefields of extraordinary size. In João Gil, a hamlet southeast of Luau, eleven out of more than two hundred people – 5 percent of the population – are amputees. Turner said that in Luau city at least 3 percent of the population are amputees, but that the true casualty rate is unknown and probably higher.

After their visit, Turner and Rice estimated that within an area nearly 4,000 kilometers square (1,544 square miles), there are at least twenty-four minefields of varying sizes. Luau's airport, fields, footpaths, water wells, and the cemetery are strewn with the weapons. At Lumege, half way between Luena and Luau, one UNITA-controlled field is estimated to contain five thousand mines.

"Luau is under siege by mines," Turner wrote in his report. "It is totally surrounded by minefields."

UNITA rebel command has the district so tightly locked that it even sealed off the international border to keep civilians and its own soldiers from escaping into Zaire. There was no one around to protest. UNITA officers, however, were exempt from their own restrictions and were seen driving new four-wheel-drive vehicles across the border into Angola.

This was a fact-finding trip, made to gauge UNITA's reaction to MAG's plans to start clearing agricultural land. The U.S. Agency for International Development will be funding a sizable part of the operation and, as a donor, wants to be assured that its money is not about to go down the drain. So in this phase of their program, Turner and Rice act as unofficial diplomats, convincing UNITA that peace under the Lusaka accord means getting rid of mines.

Turner found the UNITA commander in Luau "vague and defensive" but not flatly refusing to let teams in. "Most of the mines there are old FAPLA mines, which UNITA would be glad to have cleared, as they are an impediment to *them*," Turner says. "But they are very cagey about their own mines."

Turner, trying to build small bridges of trust between the former enemies, made a proposal to the UNITA commander: Let some of your men, who are meant to be demobilized anyway, come to Luena and be trained in mine clearance by us. No deal, said the rebel commander. Luena is in government hands. He knows that many government troops and civilians would like to settle old scores and fears that his men, even as ex-soldiers, would not be safe in Luena. His caution is understandable.

MAG did score a breakthrough, however. UNITA agreed to let MAG open a small training school inside its territory, in Lumege or Luau. Not much, but for Turner better than nothing.

"My concern is that this is a very heavily mined area with large numbers of people meant to be coming in. My impression is that it could be a catastrophe waiting to happen."

Although their optimism has not flagged, MAG eyes eastern Moxico with a sense of urgency. MAG will return, but opening Luau and Cazombo is still many months away.

Farther west, just outside Luena and not far from the wreckage of the UN cargo flight, two small boys thread their way along a path from the abandoned village of Canhengue toward the Lumege River. They can't see over the top of the dry grass. One boy carries a slingshot and in the open spaces scans the trees for birds. A year ago the boys would not have dared walk here. In two places, villagers have replaced destroyed bridges over the Lumege with rickety structures of sticks and mud; during the rainy season they are washed away and rebuilt, over and over. The boys bounce their way across a bridge and play along the bank, one taking potshots at birds, the other one throwing stones into the river, which is ten meters across here, slow-moving and clear enough to count pebbles on the bottom.

The path was safe, and the bridge safe, but now the boys are on dangerous ground. Or potentially dangerous ground, since it has not been inspected. Mines may have been laid on the bank, and in the rainy season they become mobile. They wash from fields and bridge abutments into watercourses downstream, winding up long distances from where they were originally laid. Ironically, nature's intervention ensures that even more land is taken out of production; when villagers spot a mine washed up on the riverbank or when someone is injured, they must assume that land above and below it is unsafe.

Canhengue is a focal point of MAG's efforts. Thousands of people lived in two dozen hamlets spread out on both sides of the Lumege, and the idea is to re-link the villages and make farmland available to the people who are now in Luena shelters. Some villagers have already begun rebuilding on the Luena side of the river.

Many of Canhengue's minefields are simply too big for MAG's survey teams. "We'll mark them and leave them," Turner says. They concentrate instead on clearing small areas most likely to be used for food.

Walking out of Canhengue is to travel those connect-the-dot trails on the map. When you stand in an elevated spot or at an intersection of spider-web paths, the grassland becomes immense, silent, and scary.

Stopping at one such intersection, you know at once how a local person could be seized by indecision or panic. A villager walks on because there is no way to go except back, and there is no food where he came from. There are no signposts and few landmarks other than the river, which twists and turns. The only guides to safety are footprints, and during the six-month rainy season those are erased in minutes. It's a bad place to be lost. One woman chose the wrong path here. Slivers of bone are ground into the sand, and someone has planted a stake in the middle of the path where it branches off the main trail. Had the woman survived the explosion, she probably would not have made it to a hospital even if her rescuers had had a truck. The accident happened near the only vehicle bridge across the river; UNITA blew up the bridge some years ago, and its rusting girders hang down into the water.

Turner and Rice discuss how they might get the bridge rebuilt.

Bridge construction is neither in their mandate nor in their budget, and local government has no money for infrastructure repairs. Without a proper river crossing, it's difficult to evacuate a casualty and difficult to bring in the demining teams. If you stand on a beam of the demolished bridge and visually trace the trails to the horizon, you see no sign of the modern, mechanized world.

Farther along the trail – Turner and Rice know it by heart and cover the ridges and valleys in long strides – we pass a group of women bathing at a bend in the river, and then, from the top of a rise, the expanse of Canhengue's hamlets comes to life. Men and women on foot, a few pushing bicycles, are heading from several compass points toward Luena, laden with bags of firewood and charcoal. Scattered groves of hardwoods provide the raw material for charcoal and the only livelihood for people who once farmed. There are surprised murmurs in Chokwe of "*Chindele!*" (white men), and laughter and banter as the processions squeeze past each other, creating small traffic jams on the narrow, shaky bridges. In passing, Turner cheerily serenades the women with British Army ditties, which they enjoy but fortunately do not understand. The MAG men, outlandish pink-skinned specters in their shorts and hiking boots, have become a welcome part of the scenery. From here, routes to Luena are opening. Slender shoots of commerce have started to grow.

Pausing on a hilltop, Turner points across a valley to a piece of bottom land, starkly green in the dry landscape. Women are bent over hoes, weeding a neat crop, probably sweet potatoes. Behind them, commanding the high ground and a panoramic view, sits an old FAPLA artillery position still ringed with defensive mines. The small garden is one of the beginnings of MAG's success story in Canhengue.

Although most of Canhengue's grassland has been unused for years, very little is actually mined. Fear, including a fear of UNITA troops in the hills, keeps the land idle.

"The mines are not keeping people out of here," Turner says.

Rice agrees. "I think people could live in Canhengue again now, if they wanted to. And that's the big proviso – we don't want to force them to go back. What do they want to do? It goes back to the question of, is the peace real? It has to be their decision."

Relief agencies face staggering financial burdens just getting to people imprisoned by the mines in rural areas like this. The International Committee of the Red Cross describes how heavily mined roads in one part of Angola strained its supply efforts one year at the height of the war:

> The ICRC was forced to use air transport to bring thousands of tonnes of food and seed to hundreds of thousands of displaced people in small besieged towns. Hercules heavy-lift aircraft and up to seven smaller planes were used to ferry relief supplies over relatively short distances. Although many of the flights lasted less than 15 minutes, infrastructure, insurance, plane rental, and the relatively high expense of takeoffs and landings translated into extremely high costs, accounting for up to half the total relief budget.

In 1994 and again in 1995, the World Food Program spent roughly $7 million a month to supply basic foodstuffs to Angola's war-displaced, almost all by air. Without the mines, people still would have needed help from the outside world, but providing it by road would have been much cheaper.

As we follow footprints north out of Canhengue, the hamlet of Cangungo pops up through the shimmering heat like a mirage, and it looks untouched by the war. Wading a creek that runs through a banana grove, Rice and Turner are greeted like neighbors, with shouts and waves. Rice, who once spent the night as a guest in one of the hamlet's grass-roofed huts, practices his Chokwe as Valeriano Sangria, the headman, gives us a tour. What's unusual about the place is that people are working—because they have land they *can* work. Planted in rotation, sweet potatoes sprout in raised rows next to others with withered tops, whose yams are ready to be dug. Hills of corn are woven through a mixed orchard of oranges, guava, and the bomblet-lookalike fruit I'm now told is called *mamboke*. Mangoes now the size of marbles will ripen in September. Grapes, onions, cabbage, and tomatoes round out crops enough to nearly sustain the fifty villagers.

Walls of old mud-block houses, smoothed and diminished by decades of rain, are sinking into the red earth. Cangungo was settled, Sangria says, by the Portuguese in 1942. He says that during the civil war most of the major battles raged around Cangungo, rather than through it, and that even during the siege of Luena rebels usually left the villagers and their crops alone.

By surveying and clearing the trails, the deminers opened a lifeline, but other relief agencies had not yet reached Cangungo on approaches wide enough only for foot traffic. "We need clothes, and there is sickness," Sangria says.

Cangungo reminded me of the only other place in Angola I had seen that retained some of its self-sufficiency through the war. There, oddly, the protective factor was a disease that granted the village partial immunity from outside destruction. About 200 kilometers (124 miles) north, near Saurimo in Lunda Sul Province, a missionary group in the 1930s had turned the hamlet of Camundambala into a colony for victims of Hansen's disease. Sixty years later, even though leprosy was mostly under control in Angola, government soldiers and rebels alike gave the village a wide berth for fear of catching the disease. The villagers were hemmed in by land mines and couldn't travel far, but they grew their crops unmolested. Children showed no signs of malnutrition, and tribal structure remained intact.

Cangungo, only 13 kilometers (8 miles) from Luena, survives in like fashion, a semi-isolated island. Paths to neighboring hamlets are dangerous, and the only reasonable way in or out is the way we've just come.

At the height of the fighting in 1993, a man from one of those hamlets took the chance. Cangungo had food, and he had something – no one ever found out what – to trade. He was wearing a checkered, short-sleeved shirt, brown trousers, and a pair of soft leather shoes. Just before he reached the banana trees, a mine blew him apart. People from Cangungo and from his own hamlet were too wary of the path to recover his body. His broken bones still lie where they were thrown by the explosion, and no one in the village knows his name.

Cangungo and the other hamlets of Canhengue are still mostly bare fields and crumbling ruins, but a few hundred people toughed it out during the years of siege, and a few more have come home. How long will it take to make it really safe, to convince thousands more to return?

"We're still in an embryonic stage," Turner says, after a year of clearing many kilometers of trails. "It could take another year. But we just don't know."

viii

Why Does It Take So Long?

Standing by the river bridge overlooking the spot where the woman died, you want to summon up a picture of giant machines sweeping the savannah like teams of combines through Iowa wheat, armored behemoths with intricate systems of teeth and blades and powerful chains methodically destroying Angola's deadly crop. You imagine that instead of men with garden tools on their hands and knees.

If scientists can invent mines and soldiers can lay the weapons or spread them by air, why can't machines find and destroy them?

The question nags those who have to pay for the cleanup in seventy countries. The short answer is a variant of the old cliché that wars are easier to start than to stop. Machines do exist, but they don't yet work well enough for humanitarian mine clearance. In the unending incremental war between mine and countermine technology, the deminers have been losing, their detection and removal tools decades behind the inventiveness and motivation of armaments industry scientists. "The means . . . today are slow, unsafe, and manpower intensive" is the way an official in the U.S. Army's countermine research and development unit summed up current mine-clearance technology.

Blast-resistant wheeled and tracked vehicles can pummel, plow, roll, or explode their way across minefields, but they were designed to blaze a narrow path for advancing infantry troops, not to prepare the ground for farmers coming home after a war. The machines allow for what war planners consider acceptable levels of possible casualties in battle, but more than are tolerable in a post-war civilian context.

Several countries, including the United States, are investigating or developing a wide array of sophisticated detection and destruction gadgets that use chemicals and electronics, airborne infrared spotters, lasers, side-scan sonar, and even a helium-filled light aircraft that skims the ground to take air samples. The best way to describe them is "promising."

The U.S. official, a former military engineer who has both laid and cleared mines, predicted: "Within the next five years I expect we will have cured it – not the problem of mines, but the equipment to attack the problem. Technologies will be made available to allow an earnest attempt to clean them up."

The UN is testing one German-made machine in Mozambique and several types of bulldozers and flails in the former Yugoslavia.

Huge tank-like vehicles fitted with flails or chains can thrash the ground ahead of the vehicle. The flails explode some mines, but leave some behind and beat others deeper into the ground. Other machines push or drag heavy rollers that detonate by direct pressure. As with flails, the rollers fail to destroy all the mines. Vehicle treads can tip a mine up on its edge so that the pressure plate is not exposed; the mine can later right itself.

Armored plows can clear a path, but they shove the mines to one side, reburying them and destroying topsoil in the process.

Fuel-air explosives blow up the mines by creating a high-pressure blast wave just above the ground. Other machines – one is called the "Giant Viper" – throw an explosive-filled hose over the minefield.

Nature, by following its own course, turns out to be the weapons designers' ally. The rolling grasslands and jungles of Angola and the rocky slopes of Afghanistan and northern Iraq provide safe hiding places for the small weapons. Cumbersome vehicles cannot cope with mines buried in uneven or swampy ground and are useless in the snow. The breakdown rate is high, as any farmer who uses a tractor knows and as British and American companies discovered in the deserts of Kuwait.

Destroying the mines is only the second half of the problem, and for the deminers it's the easier part. "It's finding the bloody things that's unsafe," Turner says.

Weapons engineers intend their mines to impede or channel enemy troops during combat and plan that they not be easily found or removed. Plastic components, chemical fuzes, and anti-handling devices are increasingly used to foil metal detectors and human hands. Some mines have been designed to explode when they sense the magnetic field of metal detectors. Others are designed to *fail* to explode under the sharp impact of chain flails or counterexplosives. Newer designs blow up when they detect sound waves.

While awaiting the invention of a portable tool to locate explosives, deminers relied on sophisticated versions of the metal detectors used by beachcombing hobbyists. The technology gap is familiar to frustrated law enforcement agencies and airlines around the world trying to outwit bomb-smuggling terrorists.

There is an exception, and one company has begun to narrow the gap in Africa.

Grinding their way across some Angolan roads, a few ungainly armored beasts look like serious weapons of mechanized warfare. Not many years ago the Casspirs were just that. Now, their South African operators, former special forces soldiers almost as burly in scale as the machines, like to describe the several-ton vehicles as swords beaten into plowshares. Angolans who've encountered South African warfighting gadgetry in the past could be forgiven for feeling a slight discomfort at seeing them.

The Casspirs, familiar to many viewers of television, are a product of South Africa's *apartheid* era. During years of protests against Pretoria's white minority regime, the dun-colored vehicles lumbered across the black townships of Johannesburg, Durban, and the Cape, providing transport and cover to shotgun-wielding police. South Africa, forced to turn inward during years of international economic sanctions, had developed a sophisticated arms industry and a stable of armored vehicles built expressly for border patrols and the desert wars in Angola, Namibia, and Rhodesia. The vehicles, including the Casspir, were designed to survive the blast of an antitank mine and to travel long distances at speed.

Painted white now instead of desert camouflage, the Casspirs combine their armored muscle with a fine-tuned scientific grace in parts of a former war zone where it is still unsafe to drive.

The man behind the conversion is a South African military scientist who in the 1960s helped develop some of the antipersonnel and antitank mines that were later used by the South African Defense Forces in Angola. Dr. Vernon Joynt, who heads a company called Mechem, once a subsidiary of South Africa's state arms company, adapted the Casspirs to mine-detection vehicles as the regional wars wound down, and won the company a UN contract to clear mines from power lines and 2,000 kilometers (1,243 miles) of roads in Mozambique when that civil war ended. Then the UN contracted Mechem to remove mines from 7,000 kilometers (4,350 miles) of Angola's roads. About 4,000 kilometers (2,486 miles) were cleared during the contract. In 1997, Mechem was awaiting funding to sweep more roads and a major section of the Benguela Railway.

Mechem's reinvigorated war horses make use of the one byproduct that weapons inventors have not been able to eliminate: chemical odor. The Casspir itself is little more than a giant and well-protected air sampler, an armadillo with a purpose. Dangling from the vehicles' snouts, a series of tubes vacuum the air from a six-meter strip down the middle of the road and half a meter on each verge. The samplers bottle the telltale vapor that all explosives exude, even through tarmac. On overgrown bush trails or where it is safe to walk in the track of a heavy vehicle, Mechem technicians carry the motor-driven vacuum system in a backpack and sweep in front of themselves. Each location is fixed on the Casspir's Global Positioning System and two air samples from each place are sent to two different laboratories, where they are checked by trained dogs. When a dog gets a positive reading from a vial, it signals its analysis by lying down. To be certain, the positive vial is then rechecked by multiple teams of dogs in succession. If even one dog indicates that the vial contains explosive vapor, the operation moves into a second stage.

A Mechem team returns to where the sample was taken, and dogs again take the lead. With radios strapped on their backs to receive commands, free-running dogs examine the road while human handlers control their search pattern from a distance. When the dog picks up the odor and lies down nearby, the handlers move in with metal detectors, pinpoint the mine's location, and disarm or destroy it.

For all the chemical analysis, checked and double-checked, the teams move quickly. Samples from 150 kilometers (93 miles) of road are checked at a time, and the Casspirs work in successive teams over previously cleared sections. Mechem officials say their vapor collectors allow deminers to bypass metallic battlefield junk that contains no explosive residue.

If the system works, why is it, or one like it, being used only on roads and not in fields and other former battlegrounds?

Next to inch-by-inch human search, dogs offer perhaps the most reliable way of locating mines; their ability to smell explosives as deep as a meter underground is thought to be dependable. But the animals have limitations. Their sensory powers are reduced in windy weather, they tire easily in tropical heat, and they would prefer to lie down in the shade rather than on a hot road. Dogs, which must be used in rotating teams, require intense training, as do their many human trainers and supervisors who also have to be paid.

The Casspirs and the laboratory equipment used to verify what the dogs find are expensive. And there's always the unforeseen. If a Mechem Casspir runs over an antitank mine, the explosion likely will blow off a wheel and axle without killing the car's occupants; but replacing the damaged parts halts the operation and costs five thousand dollars.

It adds up. A thousand kilometers (622 miles) of cleared road can carry a price tag of $1 million. And the technique has not yet proven to be foolproof, especially on ground that may contain much explosive material.

Mine clearance specialists are often adamant that their own techniques are the best, and Dave Turner of MAG is no exception. He believes that dogs will play a growing role in combined systems – what Joynt calls the "tool box approach" – but are not the only answer.

"I would much rather walk through an area our men have cleared than through an area cleared by dogs," he says. "Wouldn't you?"

Once Turner's teams have identified an area to be cleared, that is, one they know is mined, they hammer stakes into the ground to mark the perimeters and begin the tedious task of sweeping and digging in meter-wide strips.

Sometimes, MAG and other groups are criticized for taking too long to clear too little. In May, from an area smaller than a city block, MAG's 120 engineers removed four antitank mines, twelve antipersonnel mines, and twenty-one unexploded mortar bombs and grenades. Puny figures like these tend to alarm people, especially financial donors who think in terms of cost-benefit analysis and realize that demining costs outlandish sums of money. Turner says the tally must be seen in perspective: the land *outside* the mined area.

"The number of mines isn't relevant. Those twelve [antipersonnel] mines have denied a vast area of land. Plus, it's potentially twelve limbs saved."

In his areas, Turner walks with casual confidence. In Alto Campo, where the mine casualty rate had been about one a week, Turner quickly tramps through the fields, offering only an over-the-shoulder warning to stay inside the rows of red wooden stakes.

"This land is safe – it's been cleared by us. I'd put my own children in here." By long habit, his eyes still sweep the ground in front of his feet.

Another question arises. Since the Angolan army laid most of the mines here, why haven't soldiers traded their rifles for trowels now that the war is over?

In Luena district, Turner says, the Angolan army used to have a detachment of about forty sappers; only five are left. Turner and others say that army engineers were given only the most rudimentary training in demining. He offers this story as an illustration:

In 1995 the army was escorting a UNAVEM convoy east from Luena on a main road that the army had decided was passable. The Angolan sappers – all of them – rode in the lead truck, a big Soviet-made six-wheel drive usually used for towing artillery pieces. Just outside Léua the truck hit a mine, and the rear of the truck disintegrated. The terrified sappers jumped into the ditches, which were strewn with antipersonnel mines. A UN officer radioed an SOS, and MAG worked from Luena toward the convoy, clearing six kilometers (nearly four miles) of roads before they reached the survivors at a UN outpost at nightfall.

At daylight the two dozen casualties were loaded onto a truck, but other soldiers tried to throw their wounded comrades off so *they* could get on, one witness said. It took the convoy all that day to get back to Luena, with MAG point teams again clearing the road in case UNITA infiltrators had re-mined it overnight. In all, eighteen had been killed. Ten of the dead were army sappers who had taken no part in the emergency clearance operation.

It was a story I could relate to. A few years earlier in Malange Province, I had been trying to confirm an army report of a major battle in which many UNITA troops were said to have been killed trying to overrun a remote garrison. The local commander reluctantly agreed to let me see for myself. The colonel loaded all his sappers into a truck, and the heavily armed convoy set out nearly bumper to bumper down a road known to be mined. As on the road to Canage in Moxico Province, the verges were littered with wrecks, one of them the remains of a tractor and wagon that had run over a mine, killing a dozen civilians the year before. The sappers gazed over the truck cab at the road ahead and every few hundred meters stopped the convoy to probe suspicious spots with long metal rods. It was open country and a perfect spot for an ambush. Covering twenty kilometers (twelve miles) took three tense hours and illustrated how effectively land mines slow military movements.

When we reached the garrison, the colonel inspected and congratulated the defending troops. Most were barefoot, and about half were teenagers. I still doubted accounts of the battle. The camp was too neat. I insisted on seeing the bodies of the attackers, and the colonel put a patrol together, assigning a young soldier to lead. Walking single file across the trenches and beyond the defensive perimeter, we passed the bodies of a few guerrillas who clearly had stepped on mines. Fifty meters out, the point man halted the column and turned to the officer, having decided that disobeying an order was healthier than proceeding. "Colonel, I can't take you any farther," said the soldier, sweating profusely. "We don't know where our own mines are." The colonel was furious: at his own soldiers for not mapping their mines, and at me for having pushed the matter. My heart was pounding, and my confidence in the army's ability to deal with land mines was diminished. I vowed it was the last time I would walk through a minefield with the Angolan army.

The return trip was even more tense. The large convoy could have easily attracted the attention of rebels in the bush. The colonel, thoroughly bad-tempered behind his wraparound sunglasses and peering out of the jeep's side windows, suddenly bellowed for the driver to stop. Carefully, two soldiers began to dig near a rear wheel. I wondered how close we had come to hitting a mine. Finally, one soldier returned with his shovel in one hand and a tiny mango tree in the other. The colonel, a keen horticulturist, wanted the seedling for his garden.

For reasons of safety and strict political neutrality, MAG will not train or hire any serving member of the Angolan armed forces. The army offered to work directly with MAG in some areas, but Turner refused. MAG engineers had had no mine accidents since they began operations in 1994, and Turner decided he could not risk the confusion that might result from working with army sappers who had questionable skills. There are too many mines and too little room for mistakes.

Just outside Luena, a man-made gully called the Val once irrigated large tracts of land that helped feed the town. During the war, the army mined parts of the gully and an adjacent service road. After the fighting stopped, local officials asked MAG to clear the gully, and MAG agreed. But when army sappers tried to join in, leapfrogging over MAG's engineers, the British specialists saw potential chaos and pulled out. Nothing has been done here since, and the gully, untended and with mines washed along its banks, empties into the river during the rainy season.

Army engineering battalions overlook a lot of mines, Turner says, and even contribute to the problem by blowing up the ones they find instead of removing them. Destroying a mine on the spot is faster and maybe safer than digging it up, but the practice adds more scrap metal to the junkyard and increases the time it takes to do a thorough search with metal detectors.

The Angolan government, foreign charities, and the UN agree on one thing: demining eventually will have to become an Angolan operation. INAROE, with the UN's help, has begun training and deploying its own demining teams.

Walking past a grove of trees near the irrigation gully, Turner stops to examine an unexploded rocket-propelled grenade lying in a clump of fire-blackened weeds. The grenade, having been first fired from a launcher and then heated by seasonal grass fires, is unstable and too dangerous to move. Turner notes its location and will send someone to blow it up.

Unexploded ordnance – UXO, as it's known in the trade – is a parallel problem. The ammunition claims fewer victims than mines, but finding and removing it creates an equally time-consuming and dangerous chore.

A surprising number of grenades, mortar bombs, and artillery shells fired during combat do not explode. When projectiles contain defective fuzes, faulty circuits, or inferior-grade explosives, they lie where they fall, their destructive power dormant. They frequently explode when disturbed or handled. After battles that raged for weeks or months, parts of Angolan cities and countryside are carpeted with the ammunition. In roofless outbuildings around Luena airport, stacks of old Chinese grenades and shells lie baking year-round in the sun; the army considers them a strategic stockpile and will not let MAG move them.

These remnants are as hazardous to disposal experts as they are to civilians. When the British charity Halo Trust was clearing huge numbers of mines and ammunition left over from the year-long siege of Kuito in Bié Province, a former general in the Afghan army picked up a detonator one day. It exploded, taking off one hand and ending his career as a mine clearance worker in Angola.

The smaller of Luena's two outdoor markets spreads out along the old railway line on one side of town and on a Friday morning is packed with shoppers and traders at tables of fruit and dried fish, soap and cigarettes, and stolen medicine and clothing.

MAG engineers have been working along the railway embankment, which was once a heavily mined position on the city's inner defensive ring. They pick up or destroy whatever unexploded shells they find and rely on local people to tell them about others. That morning a boy reported one lying in the grass less than a hundred meters from the market's edge.

This time it's a hand grenade, Chinese or Russian. A soldier had pulled the pin and thrown it, but the safety lever failed to pop off in flight, and it landed with the lever down. The grenade would not need to be picked up in order to kill; it could roll underfoot and disengage the safety lever. Having lain here for several years, it's too risky to re-pin and move, so João Cayombo decides to blow it in place. Traders and shoppers are evacuated to the far side of the market while the engineer places an explosive charge next to the grenade and uncoils an electric wire a hundred meters back to a firing point. When the grenade disappears with a satisfying bang and a cloud of black smoke, dozens of children pour out of the market, cheering and dancing.

Cayombo and his team move on, up the trail to a spot where a Chinese 60-millimeter mortar shell, also a dud, has been reported in the vicinity of several houses. The shell lies inches off the main path out of

Luena; other shells will remain in the weeds until the whole area can be systematically surveyed. After chasing away several goats and children, Cayombo rigs the shell with an 85-gram block of plastic explosive and reels out the electrical cord. When another engineer presses the firing button, only the demolition charge blows. The blast cracked open the warhead, but the low-grade explosive inside is intact and, now, even more dangerous. A second try, doubling the size of the demolition charge, succeeds. These small Chinese mortar shells were notorious for their failure rate in combat and litter Angola by the hundreds of thousands.

When Turner says that he would allow his own children into a field his teams have cleared, he's probably resorting to hyperbole. Not because he's unconvinced of the safety, but because as a professional deminer he knows there is no assurance that all weapons and unexploded ammunition can be found.

During the First World War battle for Vimy Ridge in France, artillery bombardments were so intense and sustained that flat farmland was churned into rolling hills. Eight decades later, sections of a memorial park are roped off because of the buried ordnance that still works its way to the surface year after year. Caretakers use sheep to cut the grass. In Holland and other parts of Europe, and at the battle site of El Alamein in Egypt, land mines laid during the Second World War still kill civilians. As do bomblets U.S. warplanes dropped on Laos and Cambodia more than twenty-five years ago.

Can the world's war zones ever be made safe? In 1992, Dr. Joynt's operators, driving Casspirs with special steel wheels, detonated twelve thousand mines around power pylons in Mozambique in the space of five weeks. Afterward they had a barbecue and played soccer on the cleared ground to make their point. But Joynt and all deminers are quick to point out that the vagaries of both nature and man-made weapons guarantee that nothing is certain.

Walking out of one of Moxico's minefields one day, Turner related a story from his days in northern Iraq.

"There was this footpath along the edge of a minefield in Kurdistan and the path had been well used for seven years. Then one day a live mine was found in the path . . . people had been walking back and forth over it for *seven* years! I always keep that in mind when I see a path here that's well used."

Even successful clearance is at risk of being spoiled. After Mechem teams had swept a stretch of road near the River Lui in Malange Province, UN convoys began moving and several hundred trucks passed through. One day a UN truck hit a mine, killing two peacekeepers. Mechem suspects UNITA rebels of relaying a mine on the cleared road. Or did the Casspirs miss one? The answer may never be known.

The UN has set a clearance standard of 99.6 percent for humanitarian demining, although the origins of that precise figure seem buried in bureaucratic obscurity. It means that mine clearance aims to be thorough but allows for some degree of calculated risk. "We all struggle for a hundred-percent solution and we might even achieve it, but guaranteeing it is something different," said Tore Skedsmo, the UN's senior demining adviser in New York.

"I know of no accident in any area we declared we believe to be safe," Turner said. "At the end, someone *could* walk in and get blown up. There is no system in the world safer than clearing by hand, and no outfit in the world can guarantee that safety."

Angolan children make ingenious toys from bits of wire and scrap metal – highly detailed cars and articulated trucks with long handles to push them along. The most commonly available material for the miniature truck bodies comes from empty vegetable oil cans, and it's not unusual to see boys racing miniature convoys of trucks with the World Food Program logo on the doors.

On a sunny Monday in June, seven-year-old Andre Chiwesa was searching a rubbish pile near a neighbor's home in Luena for a piece of wire to make a truck. He picked up a small shiny object, and examined it for potential use. The object, a detonator or fuze from a shell or a land mine, exploded under the heat of his fingers, tearing his left hand off at the wrist. Shards of hot metal blinded him in the left eye and flayed his face and right hand.

Alfonso Derito, the boy's father and an army veteran, says that although he didn't see the device, it probably was a detonator from a Soviet fragmentation mine. Derito is sitting on an empty hospital bed as his son feverishly sleeps on a blanket-covered mattress across from him, the stump of his left hand wrapped in gauze bandage and his eyelid stitched and scarred.

"He's in Grade One," his father says.

ix

A Museum of Crutches

I had begun to study crutches. Closely, almost fanatically. How they're made, who has what types. Hardly any civilian mine victims in Moxico Province have artificial legs, but there is no shortage of crutches to look at in Luena or any other Angolan city. Even though mine amputees are a numerical minority, cities like Luena or Luanda, the capital, sometimes look like cities of one-legged people. Their tracks are all over the roads: two round dents in the sand with the print of a bare foot or a sandal in between. In central Angola, a deminer who had also worked in Cambodia once told me that there were more amputees in Kuito than any place he had ever been.

Luena's streets are a parade of crutches, mostly short ones of steel or aluminum, a few wooden, some full length. Some amputees have none and use a single stout stick, gripping it with two hands and propelling themselves along, somewhat the way a boatman poles a skiff on a canal.

Angolans who have lost both legs to a land mine cannot use crutches easily and do not get around much. From time to time you see them in low-slung wheelchairs with a hand crank connected to a bicycle-chain drive gear. The tricycle wheelchairs – a plywood seat with two big wheels behind and a smaller one in front – have a low gear ratio, which means that the driver must crank furiously to get anywhere. It burns more calories than walking but is better than going nowhere and is useful on uneven ground. Occasionally, double amputees (as well as victims of polio and spinal injuries) with no financial means have to drag themselves along the road, padding their hands, forearms, and whatever remains of their legs with part of an inner tube. They attract no more notice than a dog would.

One problem with crutches, small but universal, is the rubber tips: they quickly wear out. Chisola says hers last about a year, and then she finds someone to carve her a new pair from an old truck tire.

The tips on Maria Esther's crutches have worn through, and when she walks the slap of her foot on the pavement alternates with the sound of metal hitting concrete. Dozens of times a minute, the shock rockets up through the crutches and through her wrist, elbow, and shoulder joints. The sound is grating and the sensation must be worse, although she doesn't say so. Her eyes scan the roadside for scraps of tire, but recycling in Angola is desperately thorough and back country rubbish dumps are among the most desolate in the world. The few materials that are discarded are picked clean of anything useful almost as soon as they hit the ground.

Most amputees' crutches in Luena seem to match in height, however primitive the design, and Chisola and Maria Esther seem to have the only two pairs so badly mismatched. Their lopsided walk unevenly distributes strain on bodies meant to move and bear weight symmetrically. A veteran war surgeon told me the anomaly is leading the two women "to early arthritis and wear and tear on the joints. They are heading for an early entry into the aches and pains associated with old age."

You can see it happening. Although both women walk with a smooth stride, they rest often and admit to chronic shoulder and lower back pain.

Chisola says she has never asked the government or anyone else for another pair of crutches. "There's no one to ask," she says. The *mutilados* are part of the scenery.

I wonder if it's possible to buy crutches in Luena.

None of the relief agencies have or make crutches, no shop sells them, nor does the hospital hand them out. But wartime profiteers get all manner of luxury goods and necessities into unlikely places. During the siege of Menongue in Cuando Cubango Province, when children starved to death because farmers were penned in by the land mines, you could order a steak dinner with french fries and cold beer in a local restaurant. Today, one block from where Chisola and Maria Esther live in the railway station, you can buy cartons of Marlboros and bottles of Johnnie Walker Black Label. In the market you can buy a shiny new bicycle made in Shanghai, China, and still in its original wrapping. Crutches must be available somewhere.

I begin asking amputees on the streets. In the main market, a former soldier who lost a leg to a mine in Cuando Cubango in 1987 shakes his head. "In Luanda," he says. "If you can send money to Luanda, someone can buy them there." A medic at Central Hospital confirms it: "Sometimes amputees get sent to Luanda for crutches. You can't buy them here."

One afternoon an answer appears tantalizingly close. Walking up the boulevard from the railway station, I see an amputee a block ahead. What I actually see are his crutches, bright aluminum flashing in the sun. Catching up to the man and his family, I see that the crutches are brand new. The aluminum shanks are brilliant, the hand grips clean and matched, and the rubber tips still white and barely worn. When I ask where he got them, he looks alarmed and answers defensively. He may think I'm about to steal them. "From a priest in Lumege two months ago," he says. He was in Lumege, east of Luena, and a church group gave him the crutches, he repeats. The conversation progresses no further.

Then another glimmer of hope that this has not been a naïve pursuit. I hear that MSF Belgium, a branch of the international medical charity Médecins sans Frontières, runs a crutch-making workshop at the hospital, and amputees can simply go there and get them. Crutches are available, after all.

It's also news to Ulrich Tietze of Medico International. Since the German charity, along with the Vietnam Veterans of America Foundation, is in the initial stages of setting up a clinic to make artificial legs, Tietze agrees that it's worth checking out.

Behind the hospital, next to the wards and across from the morgue, we're directed to the workshop. It's padlocked, and we go into an adjoining room to inquire. "Yes, it's closed just now, but someone will be along soon," a man behind a desk says. "Would you like to see the Museum of Crutches?"

The attendant leads us into a single adjoining room with whitewashed walls and bare concrete floor, obliquely lit by bunker-like slit windows against the high ceiling. The windows slant triangular panes of yellow light across part of the floor and gray-shade the rest. The room echoes.

Neatly lined up and leaning against three of the four walls are ninety crutches – some singles and maybe forty pairs, although in this room "pairs" does not quite describe two items made for conjoint use by one person.

They're in all sizes. The smallest pair, floor-to-armpit hardwood struts screwed together at the bottom, would have been used by a child under the age of eight. The largest, also full-length and hand-carved from wood, must have belonged to a tall man or woman. The wooden tips are scuffed smooth, and the wooden hand grips and cloth underarm cushions are blackened with sweat and wear and still carry human odor.

Factory-made half-crutches, bent or broken, their aluminum finish dulled, stand next to others made of old plumbing pipe and the rough iron bar used to reinforce concrete. Steel elbow cups welded onto these have been sanded smooth over the years by human skin. On others, braces and arm rests are wrapped in rags, worn to dangling threads. Some have no braces at all, just a metal bar and rusted steel handle. There are crutches of part aluminum and part wood, and another pair with aluminum tops and steel bottoms. One metal pair has hand-carved tips of wood – not as good as rubber, but still a shock absorber.

In one corner sits a dusty porcelain toilet bowl, filled with hand-made black rubber tips. It's the equivalent of the museum's free souvenir shop, and visitors in need may help themselves.

No one knows if the display was meant to be a real museum, or just a storage room for old crutches that someone decided might as well be arranged tidily instead of heaped in a corner. Whoever lined them up – a hospital employee, the "curator" – may have done it out of respect for the human agony he saw stretching way back, but he probably was not thinking about tourists. Whatever the original intent, conversations begun outside the room tend to die away or turn to whispers inside, as if the exhibit was the work of a master artist just discovered in a dusty attic.

The attendant offers a partial but simple explanation. Some people got new crutches, or at least newer ones, at the hospital and left the old ones behind. Other former owners may have died.

The sound of a chain being pulled through a grate signals that the workshop next door is open.

When we walk in, I think for a moment that either the attendant has made a mistake or else I misunderstood: *This* must be the "museum" and the room we've just left was the workshop. This place certainly is a monument to something. About the size of a one-car garage, the room is a tangled mess of rusted steel, wire and sheet metal, pretzels of bent iron re-bar, water pipes with threaded elbow joints. It's a garage waiting to be cleaned out, a scrapyard waiting to be moved somewhere else. Barely visible on a cluttered workbench are an electric drill and a few hand tools. No aluminum rods, no plastic fittings, no technicians in white coats. Two Angolan men in blue overalls look miserable standing amid the rubble and give an apologetic shrug. Here, too, the explanation is simple: Bring your own materials, we'll make the crutches.

An impatiens plant in riotous pink bloom is growing out of a crack in the concrete by the workshop's front door, twenty meters from the stench of the charnel-house hospital wards.

When I make a black-humored and inappropriate crack about the museum-workshop in the presence of an exhausted MSF doctor, she vents her exasperation; MSF, struggling to feed three hundred malnourished children in a hospital annex, exceeded their mandate in the hope that a crutch workshop could somehow be launched with available materials and the spark of local initiative. There's none of either here and the doctor is trying to keep the children alive.

Later, I tell Chisola about the museum but not about the workshop. She and Maria Esther agree to go the following day, to see if one of the left-behinds might match one of theirs.

As we walk through the hospital gates the next morning, two young boys are whacking a soccer ball back and forth on a bit of sparse lawn. The ball is made of rags tightly wrapped with string. Both boys are on crutches. They are a blur of limbs as they fire the ball accurately and use their crutches as extra legs to block shots. Five girls, teenagers and also amputees, sit on a low wall, waiting for something or someone. The children do not notice Chisola and Maria Esther, and the two women do not notice them. Around back, as we sit waiting for the museum to open, two more boys on crutches walk by. One of them, Domingo Pedro Casco, says he stepped on a mine near Luena three years ago this month, when he was five years old. He has a terrific smile and big teeth. I ask him why he has only one crutch. "Oh, I left the other one home. I felt like walking with one today," he says, hopping off.

Chisola and Maria Esther examine the museum's rows of used crutches with little enthusiasm. There's no close match, no transferable parts, and the aluminum ones are well and truly worn out. But the attendant urges the women to "register," and he writes their names down on a waiting list in the event that decent crutches come available. The list is several pages long. Maria Esther picks out two rubber blocks and works them onto the ends of her crutches.

No one says much on the walk back to the railway station. I'm in a foul mood and Chisola is feeling unwell. I suppose I know what the women are thinking, although they are far too courteous to even hint at it: *Chindele*. White man from far away.

America, to Chisola, is simply a rich country with no connection to Angola. She is vaguely aware that Americans have fought wars, but doesn't know when or where. Nor does she know that the United States once pumped millions of dollars into UNITA's war effort, a small part of which killed her mother and brothers.

One morning Chisola sits on a stone wall by the grinding mill, a great roaring machine that belches up clouds of diesel exhaust and sweet-smelling grain dust as dozens of women in turn dump their corn into the hopper. The machine is slow and the queue several hours long. The women's faces are ghost-white with dust and their muscled arms heft the heavy sacks with ease. I ask Chisola what she would say, if she had the opportunity, to American women. She stares at the ground for a full minute, until I think she didn't hear the question. Then, for the first time, she looses a torrent, suddenly standing in front of a group of American women. This is what she says:

"You American women, you've never stepped on a mine as I did. Because, although there was war in America, it was not like here. The American war was men fighting men. But here in Angola, the war includes men, women, children. Old women, old men.

"That's why in your country you live well, there are no people with one leg. Here in Angola, many have died. So what we need, what we need is an end to war so that in the future we will have a good life as you have in your country."

She directs one particular message to the world's weapons manufacturers, especially the makers of land mines:

"These are the very people who are causing all this suffering. Because they made the mines and sold the mines to UNITA and to the MPLA, and that's why we're dying."

It's the end of the conversation, and she slips back into herself and closes the door.

X

Luckiest Survivor in the World

In 1983, the year Chisola was on the run and the rebels murdered her mother near Kavungo, few Americans could have pointed quickly to Angola on a world map. Jerry White could do that, and he was aware that Angola was embroiled in a civil war backed by the superpowers, but he wouldn't have been able to say much else about the country. A twenty-year-old sophomore at Brown University in Providence, Rhode Island, he was halfway through college and planning a study trip to Israel.

Jerry was born and raised in Cohasset, Massachusetts, a small town near Strawberry Point on Massachusetts Bay, where children sailed and played tennis and went to decent schools. His father owned a local ice cream company and also was president of New England Baptist Hospital, which specialized, among other things, in hip and knee replacements. His mother devoted those years to being a homemaker, later went on to get a degree in educational counseling, and then became a sculptor. Jerry, the fifth in a line of four boys and two girls, was mulling over career choices.

Although his family was Roman Catholic, he had become intrigued with Judaic studies and was equally fascinated with international relations. He wondered if it might be possible to combine the two disciplines, maybe as a diplomat, a journalist, or even a minister. He was under no immediate pressure to choose. To broaden the picture and experience his growing interest in Israel, he decided to spend a year in the country he knew only from books. When he was accepted into a one-year program at Hebrew University in Jerusalem, the only two Hebrew words he knew were *shalom* and *shekel*.

As he prepared to leave the United States that summer, Jerry White was, in his words, a typical "preppie New Englander." At six-foot-three, 175 pounds, and with a full head of black hair, he was single, handsome, physically fit, and brimming with the confidence and enthusiasm of a twenty-year-old to absorb anything new. But it was his first trip abroad, and he arrived in Jerusalem, he says, "nervously" in July. The taste of hummus, the Middle Eastern chickpea staple, and the sights and smells and sounds of Israel came as a delicious assault on the senses of a young American accustomed to hamburgers and the English language. He wasted no time picking up Hebrew and soon was nearly fluent, albeit with an American accent that brought more than a few jibes. By the end of the summer he had written an essay in Hebrew and had made new friends, both Americans and Israelis.

Israel had invaded Lebanon the year before, determined to smash the Palestinian threat to its security. Foreign students were thoroughly warned about the danger of terrorist attacks, and Jerry adopted caution as a routine part of life in the Jewish state. But the region's turbulent politics seldom intruded on university life.

The next April, after a semester of classes, he decided to take a month off and really see the Middle East. At Passover break, he and two American friends, David Kenyon from Texas and Fritz Balwit from Wisconsin, loaded their backpacks and set off for northern Israel.

For three Americans interested in combining history, religion, and breathtaking scenery, the hilly finger of land between Lebanon and the Golan Heights seemed a good starting point. The Banias had it all. Part national park and part farmland, the Banias stretches out below the southern side of Mount Hermon, near the source of the Jordan River. A spectacular waterfall and hiking trails draw tourists from around the world. According to the Old Testament, Jesus walked here with his disciples and, when Simon accepted his authority as the son of God, decided to found his church upon the rock of Peter. The Banias, named after the Greek god Pan, has been strategically important for centuries to those who either possessed or coveted it. Christian Crusaders held it in the twelfth century, and during the Six-Day War of 1967, Israel captured the territory from Syria.

Jerry and his companions spent the first day hiking and in late afternoon branched off the main track and through a wood, stopping to camp overnight on a rocky ridge with a long view.

Examining the site, the three young Americans felt like amateur archaeologists. They sensed that something had happened here.

"It had an ominous feel to it. There were bits of old walls and sheet metal, and we thought maybe it was part of an old bunker," White says, remembering the evening. "It was a curious place."

Looking through binoculars, they watched a man in a *kaffiyeh* in a field below and wondered about him.

After dark, they sat around the campfire and read aloud to each other from a book about the Six-Day War. They reckoned that the ridge had been a Syrian military position. History was close at hand and palpable.

Thursday morning, April 12, 1994, was brilliant and cool, and around nine o'clock the three shouldered their packs and set off. At the bottom of the hill they'd be able to catch a bus to the next town. The Banias was a beautiful spot, but there was a lot more of the Middle East to see.

Wearing a T-shirt and surplus army fatigue pants, Jerry took the lead. David and Fritz were about ten meters behind. It felt good to be hiking again, and they wanted to get a few miles behind them before the midday heat.

Then, in a microsecond, the world changed forever.

"The earth exploded around me in a deafening blast and I landed on my hands and knees," Jerry says. "I remember tasting dirt and smelling this fleshy, dirty, metallic smell, the smell of burning flesh."

They were in the shadow of the Golan Heights and Jerry's first thought was that they had come under rocket attack. They braced for another explosion and desperately looked for shelter. There was nowhere to hide on the open stony ground.

"I was screaming and my friends jumped on some rocks – they said 'Don't move!'

"They turned me over and I looked down and I saw I had no foot and the other one was shredded and bleeding . . . My God, I have no foot, and I started to almost chant: 'I have no foot, I have no foot.' We started screaming for help but there was no human activity there at all."

David, a premed student, put a tourniquet on Jerry's leg to stem the bleeding. Covered in blood and dirt, Jerry continually ran the palms of his hands over his hair, front to back, front to back, an unconscious gesture to calm his rising panic. As he fought to control the terror and no more explosions came, Jerry realized what had happened: he had stepped on a mine. Until that moment, land mines had been a concept outside his vocabulary.

The odd premonition of the night before had materialized into disaster: They were in the middle of an old Syrian minefield, in deep trouble and miles from help.

Jerry's right foot had been blown off at the ankle. The blast had ripped open his left calf and knee and shot large slivers of bone from the right foot into his left leg. "Like an arrow," he says. It tore gaping holes in his left thigh and peppered his face with dirt and stones.

Badly wounded, confused, and desperately thirsty, he tried to focus on his immediate plight. He wondered if his right foot, when they did get medical help, could be reattached. But when David and Fritz searched for it, all they found was a badly shredded hiking boot. The thick-soled boot had probably saved a good part of his leg.

There was no way out except through the minefield.

"We made a choice, to head toward the nearest kibbutz or town. They had to carry me, and we left all our equipment, our packs, passports, everything. They carried me, my arms around their shoulders, and my legs kept hitting the brush in front of me. I fell twice going down the hill and each time I fell was excruciating."

"We were praying every step of the way, God have mercy, and they were trying to walk on rocks or piles of rocks."

When they stumbled and fell the third time, Jerry told his friends he could not go on. David stayed with Jerry and Fritz went for help, hoping *he* would not step on a mine on the way out.

A mile or two away as the crow flies, a man in a kibbutz had heard the explosion, knew immediately that someone had stepped on a mine, and set off in his van to search. As he drove along below the ridge, Fritz staggered out of the minefield into the road.

The two men hiked back up into the minefield, trying to precisely retrace Fritz's steps. The hillside was littered with antitank and antipersonnel mines: it had indeed been a Syrian stronghold. Stepping on rocks rather than between them, it took them more than an hour to get Jerry out of the minefield – this was Fritz's third trip over the same dangerous ground – and into the van. A radio call had gone out about the incident, and at a nearby intersection Jerry was transferred to a waiting ambulance.

Despite waves of searing pain every time the ambulance rounded a curve, he never lost consciousness. Four hours after stepping on the mine, Jerry was wheeled into the operating room of a local hospital, and surgeons, hoping to save a substantial part of the lower right leg, amputated just above the ankle and put it in a plaster cast. For days afterward, the pain was so intense he could not stand to have anyone touch the side of the bed.

If a human being has to step on a land mine, Israel may be the best country in the world in which to do it.

In many countries, evacuating land mine casualties over bad roads to a first-aid post can take anywhere from six hours to several days. The delays regularly lead to death from hemorrhage or gangrene. Jerry had been lucky.

Two weeks after the operation, he was transferred to a hospital in Tel Aviv and put in a room with Israeli soldiers who were being treated for a variety of war wounds, including traumatic mine amputations.

It would be one of the most important weeks of his recovery.

"I got put in a wheelchair and I ate in a mess hall with other amputees – it was all stumps eating lunch!" He roars with laughter as he tells the story twelve years later. "I thought, 'I don't want to eat watching these people . . . the food . . . and it was all in Hebrew! I felt sick! Later there was this guy showing me his stump and taking off his artificial leg and putting it back on. I thought, 'I hate you, whoever you are.'"

Back in the ward an Israeli soldier who had stepped on a mine in Lebanon and was now walking with an artificial leg asked Jerry to guess which leg he had lost. The soldier was obviously well-pleased with his own rehabilitation.

"Then he said to me, 'The battle's up here, not down here' – tapping his head and then pointing to his foot. Then he said, 'Ach, you got a BeeKay? You got a head cold.'" BeeKay – the initials "B" and "K" – is common medical parlance for a below-the-knee amputation. "And I was thinking, I guess the guy is right – you've lost your foot, get over it." Jerry was deciding he was as tough as any Israeli combat vet.

He also had a lot of moral support. At times, too much of it. His mother had come over from Massachusetts, American and Israeli student friends were visiting, and several Danish nurses he had met earlier dropped in daily. Letters poured in from friends at Brown University.

"My room became like an ongoing Bible study. Some people were playing the guitar, some were reading the Bible, and people were bringing me lemon squares and cookies." Jerry's mother had been counseled at a local collective farm to do her crying there rather than at the hospital. Being a mother, she cried at the hospital anyway until one day Jerry uncharitably snapped: "Mother, the last time I looked, it was my foot, not yours."

The surgeons had made a good attempt to preserve his ankle but now found necrotic tissue inside the wound and told Jerry he would need a second amputation. He had reached a decision point: Should he go back to the United States to have the operation in familiar surroundings, or should he stay on in Tel Aviv? Unintentionally, the Israeli soldiers helped him make the choice.

One soldier had been horribly wounded by a mine in Lebanon. He had lost one leg immediately and was about to have the other one amputated. He was also partially blind. "He used to give me some of his grandmother's schnitzel," Jerry says. "And he gave me a hard time about being a 'stupid tourist.' Many of them had the attitude that as an American you were incredibly spoiled." The battle-hardened soldiers had taken him into their unique, grim fraternity, the hospital was clean and efficiently run, and the medical care was excellent. Jerry decided to stay.

The cookies kept coming, Jerry got taken to concerts ("One amputee in a wheelchair kept tipping over forward, and I worried that our stumps would offend other people in the theater"), and Yitzhak Rabin, then Israel's Defense Minister, stopped to shake hands when he was visiting wounded soldiers.

Self-pity was a luxury not permitted in the military ward, and Jerry had enough support to keep it at bay most of the time anyway. And the trauma surgeons preparing for the second amputation were among the most experienced in the world.

In Tel Aviv in 1984, Jerry had everything that Chisola would not have in Eastern Angola six years later.

A surgeon described in detail the likely course of the operation, using a felt-tipped pen to sketch the planned incisions on Jerry's skin. Plenty of calf muscle would be saved and used to make "a good stump," which would be crucial later on. When Jerry asked how much of the leg he would lose, another patient wisecracked that it would depend on how hungry the surgeon's dog was that day. Jerry gritted his teeth but by then could handle whatever the veterans dished out. "It was hilarious," he says. "There was a lot of joking. You knew your life wasn't in jeopardy, it was about rehabilitation and learning to walk again."

The second amputation, in early May, was performed about eight inches below the knee. As he was coming out of the anesthetic, a nurse in the recovery room reminded Jerry of a detail he had had little time to dwell on. She asked how an American civilian had managed to step on a mine, and, when he told her, snapped, "It can't be!"

What she meant was that the minefield, inside Israel's borders and seventeen years after the war, certainly *could not have been unmarked*, as Jerry claimed.

"I wanted to grab her by the throat and throttle her," Jerry says, recalling the nurse's rather stunning lack of sensitivity. Jerry insists that the minefield was neither fenced nor signposted and points out that although he and his friends had been hiking off the beaten track, nothing would have persuaded them to enter a marked minefield. His theory is that people in local kibbutzim knew about it, and backpackers usually stayed on the tourist trails.

At the time, the fact that an American had blundered into a Syrian minefield on Israeli territory was a potential embarrassment to the Israeli government. Perhaps to avoid an awkward incident with its chief foreign ally or, more probably, Jerry says, because it was the "right thing to do," the Israeli government provided him with the same insurance coverage it gives Israelis. Paying the bills, for the surgery and the long rehabilitative process that lay ahead, was not going to be a problem.

Jerry's wound healed slowly, and the ward camaraderie could not fill all the gaps in the recovery process. The gnawing pain had boredom and uncertainty as companion enemies. Parts of those long days were spent staring at the ceiling and thinking.

"It was . . . how do you pass the time? Much of the time was spent just lying in bed . . . How do you pace yourself? Is it time to get the bed changed? Time for a shot? You didn't know the future, and you often felt down. There was a humdrum side of the suffering."

Tasks like getting out of bed into the wheelchair became critically managed events focused on pain.

Jerry soon was rolling himself down the corridors, but the relatively easy mobility was short-lived. "They kicked me out of the wheelchair and gave me a pair of crutches," he says. It was time to go to work.

The crutches, like the ones Chisola would get after her second amputation, were aluminum with plastic arm braces and rubber hand grips. Learning how to walk was harder than he had imagined. Muscles and the sense of balance acquired in childhood had to be radically readjusted. And his brain had to catch up with reality: neural memory and phantom pain made him forget that nearly half of one leg was gone.

"You feel more vulnerable. They warn you that when you get up in the night you *will* take a step and you *will* fall." He did, and the pain was a persuasive teacher. "You become very protective of your stump and you will do *anything* to avoid falling."

Rehab classes began at once. "We were doing a lot of physio with soldier-therapists who were trying to break you . . . they were making you do pushups and throwing a medicine ball at you—hard. Their toughness made you feel, 'You wimp American.'"

For weeks on end, with no letup from the military instructors, civilian amputee Jerry did pushups and more pushups, lifted weights, and worked the parallel bars. He was pounding his body back into shape and getting good on the crutches.

But something else was happening, and he wasn't quite sure what it was.

"I was lashing out at people closest to me, friends, my family. I prayed: Give me the strength to get through this and not embarrass You, God. At one point I felt like I was bottoming out. Everything was confusing, emotionally and spiritually. What exactly does God do, I was thinking. Not protect people from land mines, obviously.

"I look back now and say, 'look what I had—family who came over, people baking me cookies . . . everyone should have a family! I had optimism for the future, I had hope, and I had support in a big way.' But . . .'"

The soldier had been right: It was "all up here." Jerry would have to learn how to deal with whatever was happening in his head without offending his support community.

"Sometimes the biggest thing you can do is bring someone a casserole and then go away," he says.

Jerry, although cushioned by financial security and the peculiar circumstances of his own accident, was learning the same lesson Chisola and land mine victims around the world all do: It's a lonely trip on a hard road.

Two months after he was carried out of the minefield, Jerry got his first artificial leg. It was kind of a training leg, a skeleton of the proper leg to come. As he was getting used to it, he was also getting tired of the confines of the ward. When some Israeli nurses invited him to a social gathering one evening, he sneaked out of the hospital and walked on crutches two blocks to their apartment. But as he walked across the living room to make himself a cup of coffee, his sandal snagged on the edge of the carpet and he fell. His stump, protected only by a light dressing, took the brunt of the impact.

The accident created a blood clot beneath the skin and a new wound that was slow to heal. Jerry was back to square one: in a wheelchair with a new plaster cast on his leg. The trial prosthesis that had been so carefully fitted was useless. Friends had begun returning to school in Jerusalem and the United States for the fall season and Jerry was even more on his own. When he got his first real prosthesis in August, he learned . to walk all over again.

"It was very tentative," he recalls. "I was shy of putting pressure on it and felt unstable . . . you feel you can't trust yourself." He was back on the parallel bars, learning to put weight on the leg, and having constant adjustments to make sure the new device kept his hips aligned. "They move you in baby steps. You feel a fear of the scar breaking open. It was totally bizarre. Uncomfortable. You don't know how much it [the stump] can take. The training was as hard as it had been learning to walk on crutches. "They say, 'Don't favor the leg! Don't limp! Now I want you to favor the prosthetic leg! Stand up straight!' . . . and it was all in Hebrew."

In early October, after more than five months in Israeli hospitals, Jerry headed home.

Among his friends and classmates at Brown, Jerry had always had a reputation as a bit of a jokester—witty, occasionally impatient. When he got back to New England, his friends were nervous and concerned. Physically, he was in reasonable shape, they knew. But what would he really be like?

"They were worried at first, but then they were relieved. Relieved to find out I was the same old Jerry."

He resumed old friendships, finished his studies, got married, and had children. He picked up his tennis game, learned to drive with one foot on the pedals, and became an arms-control analyst for a small private group in Washington. His sense of humor was intact and, as before, he was constantly in motion. But he was not "the same old Jerry."

His office in Washington, D.C., may not have the best view in town, but with the top half of the Washington Monument visible out one corner window, it's not bad. On this particular Monday morning, the paperwork heaped on the executive-size desk will grow higher as Jerry takes a half-day off for another appointment at the prosthetic clinic.

This will leave the office of the Landmine Survivors Network closed for the day. Ken Rutherford, Jerry's partner in the fledgling humanitarian group, is off, too, preparing for his tenth operation, as doctors determine whether his remaining foot can be saved. In 1993, Rutherford was working in Somalia with the International Rescue Committee, teaching Somalis how to apply for reconstruction loans. As he inspected a site near the Ethiopian border, his car hit an antitank mine. The explosion took off his right leg and part of his left foot. (Surgeons would be forced to amputate that foot in 1997.) When Ken and Jerry met, back in the United States, the two realized they were in a nearly unique position as American civilians who had stepped on mines. They teamed up to compile an international database on land mine survivors and their needs and to lobby government agencies and private organizations to donate equipment to victims. They mainly want to ensure that survivors in mine-affected countries are not forgotten as the world moves toward a ban on the weapons.

Jerry is now on his eighth artificial leg since the accident, and that's the walking leg, not the swim leg. Active adults need to change their prosthetic legs frequently, and Jerry goes through them like tires on a sports car.

The physical connection between the stump of an amputated human leg and the prosthesis, however sophisticated the manufactured part, is always an unnatural marriage. And Jerry's recent activities have helped neither appendage. An hour and a half of tennis a couple of times a week brings on swelling and pain, but joining an eight-mile walk to raise awareness about land mines triggered bursitis. Jerry figures he can get the artificial leg adjusted a bit to ease the pain – and get his swim leg repaired at the same time.

When he peels the rubber sleeve off his right knee at the clinic, the skin underneath is raw and red. "The swelling's down now, but if I play tennis a couple days in a row it's much more than this," Jerry tells Greg Wright, the prosthetic technician. "I've had this leg a year, and this is the first time I've had chronic pain or any problem, really."

Wright, a young man who is now as familiar with Jerry's leg as with his own, suggests some maintenance.

"Do you feel you have good contact?" Wright asks.

Jerry manipulates the leg, trying to figure out what damage he's done. It's difficult because although it hurts, he's not sure exactly where. Nerves send signals from a part of his body that's gone.

Wright is patient and avoids telling Jerry to ease up on the workouts. He also tells him again not to expect miracles from the artificial leg.

"The only perfect legs God makes," Wright says cheerfully. "Any prosthesis is only adequate."

This particular prosthesis, the one Jerry wears all day every day, is $11,000 worth of adequate. An advertising flyer for a similar leg shows a man on a tennis court in the middle of a powerful forehand shot. Legs like these are an attempt to get as close as possible to the original. The suction socket, a rubber sleeve that connects the real leg to the artificial, is the most basic part. It costs $400 and can be easily torn. The prosthesis is a mixture of carbon fiber and titanium, works like a car's shock absorber, and looks like a pogo stick. Jerry bounces up and down to demonstrate. The rubber foot on the end is made to look like a foot, fits into a shoe, and has "toes" that bend, approximating what real ones do in normal walking. His swim leg, with an "active ankle" that allows the rubber foot to flex in water, cost about $6,000.

The prosthetics industry is constantly evolving in developed countries, catering to amputees who have the financial means to remain as active as possible.

"I need a new leg about every three years and I actually look forward to getting my next leg because I know each one is going to get a little bit better," Jerry says.

At the same time, a new device means trouble. "It's a very intensive process to work the kinks out of a new leg. In the early stages you feel discomfort. So you're reluctant to change if you've got a good one. Every time you get one, it's a disappointment . . . it's always two steps forward, three steps back."

The problem is also cyclical in nature. Sharing the raising of four young children with his wife, Kelly, means that he has less time than he once had. And he can no longer walk eight miles without paying a price for weeks afterward. "The problem is that a prosthesis makes you less active, which puts on weight, and that puts more weight on the prosthesis, meaning that you have problems with it," he says.

Although Jerry has access to state-of-the-art medical care, he knows that a physical process set in motion by stepping on a mine will continue. Two or three times a year, pain forces him to shift back to crutches for awhile or stay off his leg altogether. "I'm already approaching middle age," he says. "With bursitis now, I'm starting to look down the home stretch, and I wonder what problems will come up as I get older."

As difficult and complicated as life is for adult mine victims, the problems are magnified for children, who can need a prosthesis twice a year, dozens over a lifetime, to accommodate their growing bones. In many developing countries, artificial legs cost more than $100 each, a sum that can approach the average national per capita income.

"I have been the luckiest land mine survivor in the world," Jerry says. "I'll never know what it's like for [the other victims], but I've had a glimpse of how painful and difficult it can be. Every time I'm back on crutches, it's a reminder of how vulnerable you can feel."

Jerry earns a "solid middle-class income" and lives in a five-bedroom, four-bathroom brick colonial on a half-acre in Maryland. He reckons that over the past twelve years he has spent, with the generous help of the government of Israel, close to half a million dollars on medical care and artificial legs. The expenses will continue.

Around the time Jerry was being fitted for his first plastic leg in Israel, the international Red Cross was making artificial limbs in Angola and training local technicians at a school near Huambo. In a bitter but rather typical irony, mines still concealed in the ground again compounded the difficulties of caring for victims: local forests had plenty of wood for artificial legs, but gathering the wood was too hazardous because of the mines. For a time and at greater expense, wood was brought in from the northern enclave of Cabinda until the fighting also cut off that supply.[1]

xi

"Not War, but Murder"

The invention of gunpowder increased the efficiency of killing and wounding by great leaps. Earlier methods of waging war were devastating but slow and labor-intensive. Medieval attackers trying to beseige enemies holed up inside a fortress would tunnel – dig a mine, in effect – underneath the corner of the fort, stuff the cavity with flammable material, and set fire to it, hoping to ignite and collapse the structural timbers.

Even before explosives, armies in the field found ways to deter and punish their enemies. To delay pursuers, Roman soldiers scattered an early version of the land mine, called the caltrop, a four-pointed iron spur that landed with one spike up to inflict painful wounds on men and horses.[1] Roman legions also devised effective means of denying land to their enemies. After the third Punic War in 146 B.C., Rome decreed that Carthage in North Africa would never be used again. Carthaginians were sold into slavery and the town was sacked, plowed under, and sown with salt.

Explosives were not long in altering the way battles were fought. Chinese forces reportedly laid "ground mines" and used hand grenades and rockets during the defense of the besieged city of Pien-King (the modern city of Xi'An in central China) in 1232.[2]

Six hundred years later, land mines were introduced into modern warfare – not in Asia, but in the southern United States.

During the Seminole War in 1840, U.S. Army Captain Gabriel J. Rains was learning firsthand the disadvantages of fighting Indians who outnumbered him in the flatlands of Florida. Tired of being ambushed and trying to gain the advantage, Rains booby-trapped the corpse of one of his soldiers with an artillery shell specially fitted with a sensitive fuze. During the night, the mine killed an opossum instead of an Indian and triggered a firefight in which Rains was wounded, wrote Milton F. Perry, a twentieth-century historian who chronicled the first known use of mines on U.S. soil.[3] The misadventure gave birth to a technique so deadly and unpredictable that it unnerved even its users.

Rains, something of an unappreciated military visionary, was not put off by failure. Two decades later, as a Brigadier General in the Confederate Army during the U.S. Civil War, the ordnance expert persisted with his experiments with fuzes and shells until he succeeded in establishing land mines as a weapon that served the dual purposes of defense and terror. His target this time: Federal troops blazing their way across Georgia behind the vengeful sword of General William Tecumseh Sherman. One of the first to die from a land mine was not a Union soldier, but a civilian telegraph operator who was trying to install a pole.[4]

As Rebel troops fled Sherman's onslaught, Rains perfected his mines, and Confederate troops used them in large quantities on land and, to greater effect, in rivers and harbors. By the time the war ended in 1865, Confederate sea mines had damaged or sunk forty-three Union boats and ships.[5]

The new mines, particularly the ones on land, caused outrage throughout military ranks. They also triggered a heated debate that would continue through the next century.

Despite the appalling slaughter in the first two years of the war, soldiers regarded battle as a contest to be waged by generally fair means. By 1862, land mines – known then, along with sea mines, as "torpedoes" – had added a new dimension to the miseries of fighting men.

"Their letters and diaries reveal a newfound fear – fear of a weapon they could not see or hear, a weapon that lay dormant and concealed, causing death at the slightest touch," Perry wrote. "This was different from battle; in battle a man knew what his enemy was, could hear him and often see him. This was the unknown."[6]

Union soldiers marched warily down empty roads and through abandoned Rebel positions littered with mines. Even vacant houses were booby-trapped. "They were placed upon all approaches to the rebel works [of Spanish Fort], and in every path over which our troops would be likely to pass," one Union officer wrote. "Even the approaches to the pools of water, upon which the men relied for cooking, were infected with them . . . the knowledge that these shells were scattered in every direction would necessarily produce its effect on the troops, who never knew when to expect an explosion, or where to go to avoid one."[7]

One soldier watched in awe from shore as tugs and gunboats dragged a channel for the devices, some of which resembled metal-strapped barrels with conical ends:

"Here is a monitor with a drag behind it, which had just fished up one; and the sequel is told by a bloody and motionless figure upon the deck," the soldier recalled. To put the concept into perspective, he had to reach back to his school days into Greek mythology:

"These torpedoes are the true dragon teeth of Cadmus, which spring up armed men."[8]

General Sherman, a soldier well-practiced in scorched-earth tactics and not known to be squeamish about casualties, first saw the effects of land mines on December 8, 1864, a few miles outside Savannah, Georgia, when he came upon a group of soldiers by the side of the road. One soldier, a Lieutenant Tupper, had had one foot blown off and a hand and knee mangled when his horse stepped on a buried mine.[9] The young lieutenant was waiting to have his leg amputated. The general, despite his reputation as an advocate of "hard war," was enraged:

> There had been no resistance at that point, nothing to give warning of danger, and the rebels had planted eight-inch shells in the road, with friction-matches to explode them by being trodden on. This was not war, but murder, and it made me very angry. I

immediately ordered a lot of rebel prisoners to be brought from the provost guard, armed with picks and spades, and made them march in close order along the road, so as to explode their own torpedoes, or to discover and dig them up. They begged hard, but I reiterated the order and could hardly help laughing at their stepping so gingerly along the road, where it was supposed sunken torpedoes might explode at each step, but they found no other torpedoes till near Fort McAllister.[10]

Common artillery shells that were now being used in a different way transformed the enemy into a devious, evil wraith in the eyes of Union soldiers, who accused the rebels of war crimes. In a letter to Edwin Stanton, President Lincoln's Secretary of War, Major General George McClellan wrote:

"The rebels have been guilty of the most murderous & barbarous conduct in placing torpedoes [land mines] *within* the abandoned works, near wells & springs, near flag staffs, magazines, telegraph offices, in carpet bags, barrels of flour, etc. Fortunately, we have not lost too many men in this manner – some 4 or 5 killed & perhaps a dozen wounded."[11]

Even some Confederate soldiers were horrified at the emergence of a weapon devised by one of their own. Mines were not "a proper or effective method of war," said General James Longstreet, ordering Rains to lay no more.[12]

Anger and uncertainty gradually gave way to acceptance. Land mines were unorthodox and possibly uncivilized, but they worked – not necessarily by determining the outcome of battles, but by delaying troop movements and spreading a debilitating fear. By 1864, Sherman decided that mines were "justifiable in war in advance of an army, so as to make an advance up a road more dangerous and difficult . . . But after the adversary has gained the country by fair warlike means, the case entirely changes."[13]

Sherman's forces began using mines, too, discovering in the process something that successive generations of soldiers would also find out:

land mines, unlike their rifles and cannons, claimed casualties long after the fighters had moved on.

One Union officer wrote: "The carelessness evinced by the Rebels, in marking the places of their deposit, is most culpable, as many of them could not be found, are liable at any time to injure persons, who from curiosity, or other motive, may visit the ground."[14]

Fifty years later on another continent, the internal combustion engine escalated both the pace of war and the international arms race; armored vehicles and land mine technology in the First World War set the stage for conflicts to come. To attack British tanks, German soldiers planted artillery shells with pressure fuzes much the way Gabriel Rains had in the U.S. Civil War. But these devices – the world's first antitank mines – could be easily found and removed by infantry. Antipersonnel mines were devised to prevent soldiers from tampering with the antitank mines.

During the Second World War hundreds of millions of mines were buried across Europe and North Africa. The Soviet Union alone is estimated to have laid 222 million mines, in one area at a density of 4,000 per square mile.[15]

Destructive power and special features increased with time and use. Blast mines were refined to penetrate constantly improving tank armor. Jumping mines were invented to kill more than one soldier at a time. Directional fragmentation mines evolved as a hoped-for solution to the "human wave" Chinese infantry attacks during the Korean War. And human labor in laying mines was supplemented by automation: mortars, artillery pieces, and aircraft could lay more mines faster than men.

In the 1960s and 1970s the United States scattered mines and bomblets from airplanes over Vietnam, Laos, and Cambodia in such quantities that pilots dubbed them "garbage."[16] The "scatterables" added a new dimension to mine warfare and to civilian suffering. The tiny, camouflaged devices landed in random spreads a long way from their source; their location could not be marked or monitored. Many of the bomblets, pellet-filled sub-munitions released from a "mother" bomb, failed to explode on impact and became *de facto* land mines that claimed many casualties.

U.S. Senator William Proxmire issued a warning about dropping the weapons on Southeast Asia. "Once seeded, we would lose control over these devices and they could represent a permanent menace to the civilian population, much like old land mines," Proxmire said.[17] His warning was largely ignored.

By this time, weapons engineers and military experts were well aware of an interesting phenomenon produced by mines: a wounded enemy often was more useful than a dead one. While a corpse could be left behind or fought around, a wounded soldier required the help of others to get him off the battlefield. The screams of the wounded terrorized comrades and sapped unit morale; evacuation required vehicles or helicopters and created additional chaos in rear areas, where the complicated wounds tied down a disproportionate number of medical personnel and used more blood than other wounds.

A Pakistani sales brochure enthusiastically described the benefits of one of its mines that sold for under seven dollars. The small amount of explosive in the mine would "make the man disabled and incapacitate him permanently" because "operating research has shown that it is better to disable the enemy than kill him."[18] Officials at the Pakistan Ordnance Factories reportedly have toned down their sales pitch since that brochure was published.

Whether the mines maimed or killed outright, battlefield casualties began to rise and often on the wrong side. As wars changed from series of set-piece battles to irregular conflicts with shifting or nonexistent front lines, soldiers often wound up in their own minefields or taking casualties from the stealth tactics of guerrillas.

In Europe during the Second World War, 2½ percent of all American combat deaths were said to have been caused by mines and many times more than that in certain battles.[19] In Vietnam, about 16 percent of American ground troops killed in combat—an estimated 7,400—were the victims of mines or grenades rigged to work like mines. During six months of 1968, Viet Cong and North Vietnamese Army mines and booby traps accounted for 57 percent of the casualties in one U.S. Marine Corps division.[20] And during Angola's war to oust Portugal, 50 percent of the casualties among Portuguese troops for one year, 1970, were caused by mines.[21]

Mine warfare had got a bit out of hand, and even seasoned combat veterans had mixed feelings about the weapon.

Bernard E. Trainor, who retired from the U.S. Marine Corps as a lieutenant general, barely escaped death when he tripped on a wire following a firefight in Korea in March 1952. "I heard a 'thip' as it activated a mine, and I steeled myself for the explosion that would rip off my legs. Nothing happened. The mine had malfunctioned.

"Two nights later, the Chinese tried to recapture Hill 59. Anticipating this, my platoon had installed mines to protect our position. As mortar shells rained down and automatic weapons fire swept the hill, I could hear mines detonating and shrieks of agony. The mines saved us from being overrun . . . I feel ambivalent about mines. I know they have both threatened and saved my life."[22]

Others with combat experience said flatly that antipersonnel mines are not worth the trouble they cause. Another former Marine, General Alfred Gray, Jr., had this to say at a 1993 symposium:

"We kill more Americans with our mines than we do anybody else. We never killed many enemy with mines. . . . What the hell is the use of sowing all this [airborne scatterable mines] if you're going to move through it next week or next month? . . . I know of no situation in the Korean War, nor in the five years that I served in Southeast Asia, nor in Panama, nor in Desert Shield-Desert Storm where our use of mine warfare truly channelized the enemy and brought them into a destructive pattern. . . . In the broader sense, I'm not aware of any operational advantage from broad deployment of mines."[23]

Retired U.S. Army Colonel David H. Hackworth, often referred to as the most decorated U.S. soldier alive, had hair-raising encounters with mines in Korea the same year Trainor did. Hackworth, now an author and news commentator on military matters, said he and others frequently had to patrol through their own unmarked fields and described one such patrol in his autobiography:

"Unfortunately, there was no patrol path going out. Earlier another U.S. unit had seeded the area knee-deep in antipersonnel mines without keeping a record of where they were buried. Their short-term protection meant only long-term agony for subsequent units, who had to find uncharted mines the hard way. It was a problem that had confronted infantry since the introduction of mines, and now it was ours."[24] The mission, through what Hackworth calls "that uncharted maze of death," took three hours and left him soaked in sweat. "We'd cleared ten mines and my gut ached as if I'd done a thousand sit-ups. It wasn't work to keep you young."[25]

On another patrol, Hackworth and other soldiers were ordered to clear a path through one of their own minefields; a "Bouncing Betty" mine killed a buddy standing next to him.[26]

But Hackworth's best land mine story may be this one, in which his unit, well supplied and adequately supported by artillery, faced a "human wave" onslaught:

"Out in front of our position we laid a carpet of mines and flares. The enemy attacked in regimental strength, outnumbering us 9 to 1. They walked through our minefield – and our gunfire – without missing a beat. They cut my company in half and within an hour were two miles to the south, in our rear. The only way out was to move north, so we trudged through our own somewhat depleted minefield to escape, losing two men in the process."[27]

Citing his experiences in Korea and Vietnam, Hackworth says that neither his units nor the enemy were ever seriously deterred by mines, and today he has no question about the military utility of the weapon: "I've never seen a battle in which land mines made a difference to the outcome. They are ugly and ineffective weapons, and they ought to be outlawed."[28]

Growing uneasiness about battlefield "own goals" and questions about mines' effectiveness against an enemy led to more research. Military technology, like nature, constantly seeks to fill a vacuum or improve existing designs. These are just a few types of mines developed since the Korean War to maim or disable enemy personnel or machines:

- U.S. AIR-DROPPED antipersonnel mines that shoot out a web of trip wires when they land and arm themselves. Some are mini-bounding mines that jump off the ground to explode when the wire is tripped. Vietnamese called an early version the "spider mine."
- THE SOVIET PFM-1, or "butterfly," which resembles an overgrown seed pod from a maple tree and is dropped from helicopters or fired from mortars. Copied from an earlier U.S. antipersonnel mine, it was used extensively in Afghanistan, where it was dubbed the "green parrot." The camouflaged, plastic-bodied mine (it comes in green, tan, or white) weighs just seventy grams and has a delay mechanism that arms it after fluttering to the ground. When the thicker "wing" of the mine is squeezed, the detonator sets off the mine's liquid explosive. The mine cannot be disarmed.
- "HUNTER" MINES, ALSO AIR-DELIVERED, with electronic sensors that relay information to a command station or to other nearby mines about sounds of vehicles, approaching footsteps, or even a helicopter in flight, interpreting "blade flash" signals from the aircraft.
- MINES THAT TURN THEMSELVES off or self-destruct at prearranged times or on command – "smart" mines, in the current jargon.

Although no mine has been invented that can tell the difference between a soldier's foot and a civilian foot, some militaries and weapons scientists maintain that the "smart" mines can prevent unwanted casualties. Many of these rely on simple batteries. When the battery dies of its own accord, the mine is neutralized. According to one U.S. army officer, 99.9 percent of the "scatterable" mines with self-neutralizing or self-destruct mechanisms would function as designed.

The "smart" mines, which first appeared in the 1960s, are still not quite smart enough, many experts say, and, like any electronic gadget, they fail for a variety of reasons. For one thing, batteries often last long beyond their predicted shelf life.

"The more complicated they are, the more can go wrong with them," says Dave Turner of the Mines Advisory Group.

Eddie Banks, the former head of the UN's demining unit in Angola, agrees that current technology leaves room for improvement. "The military research and development figure for failure rate [on 'smart' mines] is between 5 and 8 percent," he says. "The actual failure rate is very difficult to find out, as it's a secret well guarded by all countries. But in Kuwait, the failure rate was estimated by some experts to be between 70 and 80 percent."

Banks and anti-mine campaigners point out that even when failure rates are whittled down, "smart" mines still have to be removed from the battlefield. If only a few fail to neutralize or destroy themselves at the appointed time, people still will refuse to use the land.

Tore Skedsmo, the Senior Demining Adviser in the UN's Department of Peacekeeping Operations, sums up the "smart–dumb" debate this way:

"Smart mines used properly will probably save some or perhaps a lot of civilian legs after a conflict. However, why should they be used properly when all other mines are used improperly . . . Whatever failure percentage you believe in, above zero percent, would you enter a field where a number of 'killing machines' are hidden and somebody told you that they most likely or perhaps 'should' have switched themselves off by now?"

Some military planners argued that the weapon still has an important military role and that the development, already well underway, of new generations of mines is justified.

"Even with relatively costly new technologies, land mines are an affordable weapon for the entire range of military organizations, from terrorist groups to large, well-equipped armies" and "will continue to be a significant element in armed conflicts at all levels of intensity well into the foreseeable future," the U.S. Defense Intelligence Agency said in a 1992 report.[29]

Years after that report and looking ahead to wars of the twenty-first century, systems planners said the logic was still sound. Remotely delivered "smart" mines with "near zero" failure rates will be indispensable as budget constraints shrink the size of military forces, they said.

"Responsible use of mines can protect U.S. forces and speed victory and the cessation of hostilities," said Frederick J. Charles, a retired U.S. Army colonel with long experience as a combat engineer in mine–countermine warfare, including in Vietnam. "Dumb antipersonnel mines ought to go . . . for the simple fact that they are difficult to use safely and pose a continuing threat to all, friend, foe, or noncombatant. Antitank and anti-vehicle mines should remain in U.S. inventories."

Charles, now an analyst with a private corporation that makes recommendations to the government on military matters, agreed that "dumb" mines pollute whole countries and deny land to many people, but he questioned whether outlawing antipersonnel mines would work:

"Pursuing a ban of antipersonnel mines is a noble objective, but it ought not include delayed munitions with a set life less than some reasonable period of time. We should support international efforts to coerce renegade nations and irregular factions who use mines indiscriminately, violating international humanitarian law . . . There's no easy solution, because irresponsible people are still going to do irresponsible things."

He had a point, already noted in parts of the world: the older weapons may pose problems for their users, but they are effective at sowing terror and are a seductive method of warfare. "Dumb" mines are also cheap—as little as three dollars each—while self-neutralizing devices fetch fifty dollars and up. Poor countries and renegade forces will have little incentive to buy "smart" mines when they can use the dumber but cheaper "perfect soldier."

xii

The Campaign to Ban Mines

The rest of the world finally began to take note of the effects mines were having in poor countries.

The World Health Assembly warned as early as 1981 about the health effects of leftover mines and "the resulting loss of life and the mutilation and disfiguration of civilians and the other dramatic effects on agriculture, transportation, housing, oil and mineral resources, development planning, and development itself."

Libya may have been the first nation to complain about land mines as a public health issue, at the World Health Assembly in 1990. In a submission entitled "Mines laid during wartime and their adverse effects on health and people," the Libyan delegate demanded that countries that laid mines across its North African desert territory during the Second World War remove them. At the time of the meeting, though, Libyan leader Moammar Qaddafi was an international pariah accused of sponsoring terrorism, and his delegate's plea, dripping with florid rhetoric and visions of persecution, attracted little sympathy.

Soon, however, humanitarian agencies were using phrases like "public health catastrophe" and "worldwide epidemic" to describe what was happening.

Epidemic was the right word. Doctors in several countries went public with their frustrations at treating victims of this peculiar weapon, which had been designed to target specific parts of the body. Dr. Hans Stirnemann, a sixty-eight-year-old surgeon, wrote that while he had seen much during his professional career, land mine wounds were in a category apart:

"When we got new patients, my hope was always for gunshot or shrapnel, or other 'normal' war injuries, but not mine injuries, because they are the worst you can imagine. And if they were mine injuries, I hoped: please God, let it be an adult with only one leg blown off, not two legs and hands and eyes. And please God, no children coming from the fields. With ordinary war wounds, I often felt sad or furious. With children without legs, hands, and eyes, I felt not sad but sick."[1]

As the world shook off the icy grip of the Cold War, human rights and medical aid groups in the early 1990s were able to focus international attention on a subject that had gained scant specialty interest before. Initiated more or less jointly by six groups – Handicap International, the Vietnam Veterans of America Foundation, Human Rights Watch, Medico International, Physicians for Human Rights, and the Mines Advisory Group – the international campaign to ban mines chalked up rapid successes that surprised veteran peace campaigners and government officials alike.

With the support and urging of the United Nations and numerous other groups, the campaign compiled a weighty roster of countries that agreed that the production, stockpiling, use, and sales of the weapon should be outlawed. More than forty states, led by Canada, supported the ban and nearly thirty either renounced or suspended the use of mines by their own forces. In addition, more than seven hundred humanitarian charities and nongovernmental organizations in more than thirty countries supported the ban. The numbers would continue to grow.

But some countries hedged.

Although the United States had imposed a unilateral, renewable moratorium on its export sale of mines as early as 1992,[2] Washington's policy on the use of mines by its own armed forces proved to be another matter. While deploring civilian casualties and the economic disruption caused by the weapon, the Clinton administration announced in May

1996 that the United States "will aggressively pursue an international agreement to ban use, stockpiling, production, and transfer of antipersonnel land mines with a view to completing the negotiation as soon as possible."

In other words, not quite yet.

The United States would no longer use "dumb" mines after 1999, the White House said, except in the Demilitarized Zone separating the two Koreas, but would reserve the right to keep using "smart" mines until alternatives are found. Conceding a problem of global scope, the President also directed the Department of Defense to research alternatives, improve mine clearance techniques, and expand humanitarian demining programs.

Condemnation of the White House statement and the U.S. slow-track approach was swift. How can other countries be persuaded to give up antipersonnel mines while the United States says it must be able to use some types under some conditions, the critics asked.

"This policy is an attempt by the Pentagon to keep using an indiscriminate, exceptionally cruel weapon that does not belong in the arsenal of civilized nations," said U.S. Senator Patrick Leahy of Vermont, a longtime anti-mine campaigner.[3]

Former soldiers began to weigh in on the side of the argument that the weapon is not militarily useful. Fifteen retired high-ranking U.S. officers declared: "Given the wide range of weaponry available to military forces today, antipersonnel landmines are not essential. Thus, banning them would not undermine the military effectiveness or safety of our forces, nor those of other nations."[4] Among the signers of the declaration were General Norman Schwarzkopf, the commander of Operation Desert Storm; General David Jones, a former chairman of the Joint Chiefs of Staff; and General John Galvin, the former Supreme Allied Commander in Europe.

Separately, but also demanding a ban, military experts from nineteen other countries[5] judged antipersonnel mines to be of questionable value, indiscriminate in their effects, and hard for even professional armies to control. The experts all endorsed the conclusion of a study commissioned by the International Committee of the Red Cross:

"The limited military utility of AP [antipersonnel] mines is far outweighed by the appalling humanitarian consequences of their use in actual conflicts. On this basis, their prohibition and elimination should be pursued as a matter of utmost urgency by governments and the entire international community."[6]

However, some soldiers stuck by the old argument that a categorical ban was the thin end of a wedge that would weaken a legitimate military force. Bernard Trainor, the retired Marine, called restrictions on international sales a "worthy goal that could save lives. But we cannot wave a magic wand and do away with mines entirely. American troops often depend on them, and an international ban would not prevent other forces from using them. . . . Trying to outlaw mines is much like trying to outlaw war itself, an exercise in futility."[7]

Efforts to outlaw certain weapons and regulate some battlefield conduct have not always been futile. Exploding bullets were prohibited under the Declaration of St. Petersburg in 1868; expanding bullets – "dum-dums" – were banned by the Hague Convention of 1899, and together with the Hague Convention of 1907, prohibitions were placed on weapons that would cause "superfluous injury" or "unnecessary suffering." After the horrors of poison gas warfare in the First World War, gas was banned in 1925. The prohibitions on the three specific weapons have been largely respected, except for the use of poison gas by Iraq in recent years.

Since 1949, international humanitarian law has been consolidated under the umbrella of the generally accepted Geneva Conventions and two added protocols to those conventions. The 1977 Protocol declared that the right of warring parties "to choose methods or means of warfare is not unlimited" and prohibited "indiscriminate" weapons.

The most recent addition to the body of law is the tongue-twisting 1980 "Convention on Prohibitions or Restrictions on the Use of Certain Conventional Weapons Which May Be Deemed to Be Excessively

Injurious or to Have Indiscriminate Effects," usually referred to as the Convention on Conventional Weapons, or CCW. Sixty-three countries, including the United States and Canada, had ratified it by early 1997.

The CCW attempts, feebly, to regulate booby traps and land mines by stipulating that they must be used only against military targets, that their location be mapped, that air-dropped mines must be able to neutralize themselves, and that states must try to clear them after a conflict.

But the law is weak on verification procedures and other details. Overall, according to the United Nations Department of Humanitarian Affairs, "the CCW has had little or no effect on the use of anti-personnel mines in recent conflicts." A 1996 review conference did little to strengthen the convention, beyond adding that it should apply to internal conflicts. In the analysis of the International Campaign to Ban Landmines, the review "will not make a significant difference in stemming the global land mines crisis." (The conference did score one major and unexpected success by banning blinding laser weapons, which have already gone on the market in at least one country.)

In the view of the campaigners, the answer is simple: Although precise definitions of adjectives like "superfluous" and "unnecessary" have not yet been codified into law, antipersonnel mines are already illegal. Chisola Pezo and Jerry White and others around the world who lived to tell about stepping on land mines also see no need for further debate or definition.

Some health workers took the argument a step farther, arguing that it was time to look beyond the issue of land mines and rein in all arms technology. Robin Coupland, a Red Cross surgeon who operated on hundreds of mine victims in Afghanistan and Cambodia from 1987 through 1994, proposed that governments start looking at the effects of all weapons as a means of limiting weapons of the future.

If wounds could be medically classified and shown by definition to cause "superfluous injury" and "unnecessary suffering," Coupland suggested, doctors and lawyers would have a tool to pressure governments to stop the development of future weapons before they got off military drawing boards.

"In this way, a weapon universally regarded as abhorrent might not even get to the development stage through lack of funds if designers and politicians knew that the effect was already prohibited," Coupland wrote in *The Lancet*, a prestigious medical journal published in Britain. "Once documented, those who are responsible for the decisions about design and use of weapons cannot say that they are unaware of the human implications of their decisions," he added in a lecture to The Royal College of Surgeons of Edinburgh.

Coupland's proposals on behalf of the Red Cross to medical associations in Europe and North America began to attract support among doctors who supported the ban on land mines.

"The problem is that as doctors we've not done anything to stop the development of weapons when we have to treat the effects of weapons," said Dr. Vivienne Nathanson, the head of Health Policy and International Affairs at the British Medical Association.

"Many of us would like to say that all weapons are unacceptable because anything that inflicts harm on human beings is appalling. But if we can't persuade people not to use weapons, then we might as well persuade them to limit them."

William Arkin, a Vermont-based human rights consultant who specializes in weapons issues, said that the concept of addressing the health effects of weapons could be useful. "I hope it will help smoke out more data from the militaries, including the U.S., about weapons design," he said. "It could give us insight into new things."

However, Arkin thought it "a bit naive" to believe that prohibiting the effect of a weapon could result in future bans. "To think that you can reduce it to one type of weapon and say it's bad . . . that's not the way the world works," he said.

Arkin, who played a major role in achieving the international ban on blinding laser weapons, takes a hard-nosed approach to arms control.

The only way militaries can be convinced not to develop or use a weapon, he said, is by convincing them the weapon is not really useful on the battlefield.

Mine clearance experts add that a ban, while helping to put antipersonnel mines in a category of stigmatized weapons like poison gas, will not eliminate the millions of existing mines ready to be dumped on the international black market.

"If they were banned today, there will still be an impact for a hundred years," said MAG's Dave Turner. "The stockpiles are going to be causing problems for that long."

Once they leave the factory, land mines, along with other weapons and munitions, flow through discreet and well-protected channels. About one hundred companies in fifty countries manufacture mines, and the weapons' movements around the world are nearly impossible to track.

"The arms trade is shrouded in secrecy, and trading in mines is no exception," the UN's Department of Humanitarian Affairs said in an educational primer on the subject. "The exact numbers cannot be determined because rudimentary devices can be produced easily without being registered, licensed, or declared, and even sophisticated mines can be copied in other countries or produced in secret. When the export of mines from one country to another is banned, producers often deal through intermediaries or set up production in third countries to circumvent regulations and avoid public opposition."

The Arms Project of Human Rights Watch in 1997 listed nearly fifty U.S. companies that make either antipersonnel mines, their components, or the systems that deploy them in the field. Project researchers predicted that more U.S. companies would be discovered and added to the list.

"Six of the forty-seven have overseas parent companies," Andrew Cooper of the Arms Project said. "Two of the parent companies are in Germany, two are in Japan, one in Hong Kong, and one in Norway."

Arms Project researchers compiling a database of producers around the world find the task a bit like squeezing a balloon.

"We are just beginning to scratch the surface of international production," Cooper says. "It is a very nasty business. As some of the factories shut down in western countries, we suspect they're relocating to developing countries."

Land mine designers and manufacturers, whatever their nationality, do not give interviews. But Eddie Banks, the former UN demining chief in Angola, is well acquainted with the development process. Banks, who once laid mines as a British soldier and later in his career helped design high-tech "smart" mine fuzes for a commercial company, described it this way:

"The antipersonnel mine is usually designed by the military, committee-style. They write a requirement, saying what they want the mine to do, how it's to be delivered, how it's to be transported, the size, whether it's to be used above ground or below ground, and so on.

"Then it usually goes to nonmilitary people who have no concept of what a mine does. They have an electronic or mechanical background and deal with things like centrifugal force in air, how it would impact on a target. They switch themselves off from the realities of life, which is that it is designed to kill or maim."

Eventually, the mine becomes a product to be marketed.

In a series of sales flyers of "Engineer Equipment" handed out at international arms shows, the Federal Directorate of Supply and Procurement, the state arms company of the former Yugoslavia, advertised one of its most popular items, the PROM-1 jumping mine:

"The antipersonnel fragmentation, bounding type mine is intended for annihilation and incapacitating of live force by the action of fragments of the mine body. Laid individually, in groups or in minefields. May be laid in any ground, in snow, and in water to 0.5 m water level."

The catalog description, complete with cutaway engineering drawings, outlined on subsequent pages the mine's attributes ("Lethal action in a diameter to 40 m and vulnerable effect to 50 m . . . bursting at 70–80 cm from the ground"); how its fuze, booster, propellant gases, and firing pin work; and, finally, even showed how to dig holes for the mines on flat ground or hillsides.

The advertisement concluded with the Directorate's Belgrade address and telephone numbers and helpful information for prospective buyers: "Mines are packed per 10 off, with all the pertaining parts in a wooden case. The case mass with mines is appr. 43 kg."[8]

Outside Sangondo in Angola's Moxico Province, MAG's Dave Turner walks quickly through the dry grass but takes care to stay within the lines of red stakes. On the side of the trail lies one skull and the shattered ribs and long bones of a three-man UNITA patrol who tripped a bounding fragmentation mine, probably a Soviet-made OZM-72. It works the same way as the Yugoslav mine. Or another one made and aggressively marketed in the past by an Italian company. When the mine's trip wire is pulled, the detonator fires a primary charge that propels the mine body out of the ground to waist height. There, when the cylinder reaches the end of its short wire tether, the main charge explodes, throwing out two thousand pieces of sharp-edged metal that will kill anyone within twenty-five meters in any direction. It is one of the deadliest weapons in the catalog of land mine warfare and one of the most difficult to remove.

A few meters away from the skeletons of the soldiers, another bounding mine killed an entire family at once – a woman, a man, and a child – as they picked mangoes.

The Angolan army and UNITA frequently placed mines around trees, Turner says, to deny their enemies shade and food. The connection between the fruit and hungry civilians was seldom a factor in operational decisions.

That same year in Croatia, about 8,000 kilometers (5,000 miles) north of where the rebels and the family died in the orchard, Corporal Mark

Isfeld was clearing land mines one rainy October day. Isfeld, then a twenty-nine-year-old Canadian combat engineer serving with UN-PROFOR, the United Nations Protection Force in the former Yugoslavia, was pained by what the war had done to a piece of Europe.

"From my eyes, Croatia is a terrible scar on a once beautiful face," he wrote in a letter to a Canadian reporter. "I have seen churches possibly 500 years old in ruins. A monastery with breathtaking architecture; fruit trees and grape vines fill a courtyard where human voices are gone. I can almost imagine priests gathering grapes to make the wine for their communion. The church has a tall steeple with a stunning mosaic on the front. A clock hangs from the other side, but time has stopped for this ancient, sacred place of worship. Devils of war have made this treasure of history a worthless eyesore."

The soldier's letter continued: "In Croatia, where no one trusts soldiers of any sort, they see us as some sort of trouble, but I will keep on doing my duty of protecting nations that wish for peace . . . At the moment I am traveling from infantry checkpoint to checkpoint and teaching private soldier and officer alike about the mines (anti-personnel and anti-tank), unexploded ordnance, and booby traps that are still too frequent. We stress that one engineer has died, a well-trained man. As well, one (corporal) infantryman who stepped outside an area that was clear lost his foot."

When Brian Isfeld, Mark's fifty-seven-year-old father, spells his last name for a reporter, he automatically does it military fashion: "India-Sierra-Foxtrot-Echo-Lima-Delta." Isfeld is proud of his own thirty-two years in the Canadian Forces and even prouder of his son. He keeps a copy of this letter in his jacket pocket.

Standing on a street in Ottawa, the father picks up the son's story: "They were a team of deminers, and Mark was guiding an armored personnel carrier up a berm where they were repairing a water pipe in Sector South near Split, clearing this berm along a canal. The carrier hit a wire and set off a bounding mine, which was linked to some other mines. It blew his legs off. They revived him, packed the wounds the best they could, and choppered him out to Knin, to the Czech hospital there, but he died in the operating room." It was June 21, 1994, two months into his third UN peacekeeping tour. Two other Canadian soldiers were wounded in the same incident.

"I support what he was doing and have no animosity toward the military or the country for his death," Mark's father says. "He got killed doing a most honorable job. We never think it's going to happen to us. I feel very proud of my son for what he did and for his service, and I am doing what I can to perpetuate his memory, to save someone else's life.

"He shouldn't have had to die, because mines are insidious and should not exist. But I know that if Mark were alive, he'd do it again because he had a great feeling for the elderly and the very young and the helpless."

Carol Isfeld, Brian's wife and Mark's mother, crocheted little dolls back in Courtenay, British Columbia, and shipped them to Croatia, where Mark would hand them out to children, "an excuse for a hug," she says. Some of the dolls were girls in pigtails, others boys in UN baseball caps or blue berets, sewn on at just the right angle. She still makes the dolls, which now carry a small memorial tag about Mark, and gives them to other peacekeepers to distribute.

Isfeld talks about his son a minute longer and then looks up the street toward the Canadian parliament buildings. "The clichés don't wash with me. Time doesn't heal. It dulls, but it doesn't heal. Just talk to me. And let me talk. You don't have to say anything except you're sorry for what happened."

On the third floor of the Canadian War Museum in Ottawa, Mark's name, rank, and unit number are tenth on a list on a black granite stone under the inscription "Dedicated to those Canadians who gave their lives in the service of peace while serving with UNPROFOR." A sign says that more Canadian peacekeepers on active duty have been killed by mines than by any other cause.

Mark Isfeld was thirty-one.

xiii

"All I Want to Do
Is Drive a Truck"

Snapshots.

The kindest thing that can be said about the "Experiência" is that there's only one of them.

Anyone boarding Luena's lone city bus will appreciate the irony of the Portuguese word, which can mean either "experiment" or "experience," printed in the destination slot on the front. The grime-coated "Experiência," with its cracked and bullet-riddled windshield, spends most of its working hours puffing clouds of black exhaust while the few passengers sit dismally inside or push from behind trying to get its aged and fouled engine going. The bus occasionally manages to trundle across town, but most Luenans find it faster to walk.

Amputees almost always walk anyway. Just after dawn on a Sunday morning, Chisola sets off for church in the Luena *bairro* of Cazombo Dois, named for the district capital near her old village of Kavungo. It's a forty-five-minute trip each way and she does it once or twice a week. There are churches in Luena, but Cazombo Dois offers a weekly re-union, a link to the past, and an escape from the dreary confines of the railway station.

Wearing a blue blouse, bright Zairean *chitengi*, and one red plimsoll, Chisola leaves the baby in the care of her older children and walks up the long boulevard under the canopy of eucalyptus trees with Isabella, a longtime friend from Kavungo.

As they go, the women talk about the same things they always talk about: the war and money.

"They say the new half-million *kwanza* note will come out soon," Isabella says.

"The old notes will be worthless," Chisola replies.

"They're worthless now, and the new one won't mean much."

They wonder if they have enough for the Sunday collection plate. Between them, the greasy tattered notes amount to about ten cents. Why give money to the church?

"They helped me when I was in the hospital," Chisola says.

Past the smaller of the city's two markets, the road turns to dirt and then to a track of fine sand. The crutch tips sink in with each step, and her pace slows.

At the church, just after eight o'clock, it's clear why people, even amputees, walk miles to get here. In spite of the bullet holes in the walls and the shot-out windows, the church, once a school, is a minor sanctuary in a grove of mature mango trees. The hand-hewn wooden pews soon fill up.

Cazombo Dois church is also a religious fable of war. In a congregation of about fifty women, children, and men, at least five are amputees. One of them is Chisola's first cousin, who also lost a leg to a mine. Others were her neighbors in Kavungo.

Henrique Ferreira Cardoso, the church secretary, stepped on a mine in 1984. In a neat gray suit, with his left pant leg pinned up above the knee, he tucks his crutches under his arms to strum the guitar and sing a hymn suggesting that people are better off loving what is to come in heaven rather than what they have on earth. No one in the congregation would find fault with the message. The phrase "Deus & Amor" is chalked on the blackboard behind him.

The minister, an older man, has both legs, but his eyeglasses don't work too well – nothing to do with the war – so he borrows a pair and reads from the Old Testament about the crucifixion and the resurrection. The multilingual service switches back and forth between Luwale, Chokwe, and Portuguese.

Afterward, Cardoso and several others ask only one thing of a foreign visitor: Please tell our stories.

On the way back to the railway station, carrying the Bible she cannot read, Chisola is singing.

This is a picture of almost-peace, with land mines in the background.

The next Saturday, in the afternoon, a small Antonov cargo plane lands at Luena airport carrying some of Angola's last fighters. Fifty-five well-muscled UNITA rebels, eyes hard as flint, file off the plane carrying worn AK-47 rifles, a few grenade launchers, and ragged rucksacks and smoke-blackened cook pots. They're in faded and torn fatigues and cracked leather army boots wired together at the seams. Some are barefoot. One wears a T-shirt emblazoned with Mickey Mouse in U.S. combat uniform with grenades hanging off the webbing. The men smell of sweat and weathered canvas.

This is the first time the rebels have been on Angolan army territory except during battle, and they are wary as they sit in a hangar waiting for the UN trucks that will take them to quartering areas. There, the former rebels will either be integrated into the new combined army, or demobilized and returned to civilian life. A platoon of armed Brazilian UNAVEM troops watches over them protectively, while curious Angolan troops, their former enemies, watch with maybe something else in their eyes. Several of the fighters have small children with them. No one has eaten for three days.

The men are free, but there's an unmistakable prisoner-of-war atmosphere in the hangar. The men sit, their guards stand, rifles pointing outward against possible attack. Angolan army Brigadier Rafael roars up in his Range Rover, hops out, and throws his old enemies a casual half-salute.

"Don't worry, we're all Angolans, sit down, take it easy, there'll be transport for you soon to Lumege," Rafael says. As a UN officer assures the UNITA troops that they will be safe on the trip on government-controlled roads to the quartering camp, Rafael cannot take his eyes off the ragged guerrillas. A scar down the side of his face stands out against tightened jaw muscles.

One soldier in his mid-fifties says he has been in the bush for twenty-two years, fighting the Portuguese first, then his fellow Angolans. "All I want to do is drive a truck—as a civilian," he says. His smile passes from man to war-tired man.

UNITA Captain Aurelio Benguela says that most of the older men have been in the bush that long. They hope the war is over for good.

"I feel I'm free because we have been fighting for a long time," Benguela says. He hesitates and looks at the brigadier, whose expression offers less than peace and reconciliation. "But we need the UN [peacekeepers] to stay a bit longer."

One soldier sits in a battered canvas camp chair. His son, who's about three, stands between his knees watching the proceedings wide-eyed and holding onto his father's pant legs with tiny hands. The boy, born in a bush camp during the war, has no reason to believe in anything except violence and danger. Is the war over? I ask his father. "No, it isn't over. . . . there are some things missing," he says. What things? "We'll see."

Unarmed for the first time in many years, the men hold the hands of their children and climb into canvas-topped trucks for the hundred-kilometer (sixty-two-mile) trip to the quartering area.

That day's journey went off uneventfully, but a similar trip weeks later did not. Fourteen kilometers (nine miles) out of Luena, a UN truck carrying another batch of former guerrillas and their families hit an antitank mine on a road that had supposedly been cleared. Thirty-five men were wounded in the explosion. Some reports said the mine had been overlooked during a clearance operation, others said government renegades had relaid the mine after the minesweepers had passed. It was an incident the shaky two-year-old peace process did not need, and peacekeepers held their breath. A single landmine, possibly buried years earlier, could easily have reignited the war.

Donor groups who pay for demining operations keep snapshots like this one on their desks.

Successful mine clearance in any country "needs a demonstrable peace, something that will restore confidence in all the people," Dave Turner said later. "Civil wars are always the hardest to end."

Confidence is in short supply among people who have lived through more than twenty years of war.

"I have no hope that I will live better in the future," Chisola Pezo says one morning, as she sits in the railway station's sunny forecourt. "The politicians in Angola . . ." She makes an up-and-down motion with one hand. "I just want the politicians to make peace. Maybe it'll be better for my children. But I'll be very old then."

This woman, who has never been to school and never been consulted by anybody about anything, has no doubts about what causes war and how to end it. The subject may be the only one that brings her anger to the surface: "If you stop giving them guns and land mines, then they'll stop fighting. If you don't stop giving these things, they won't stop."

Maria Esther Musa, Chisola's friend of thirty years, sits down on a small stool, laying her crutches alongside. She nods but has little to add. Conversations with land mine victims in rural Angola tend to be short and to the point.

"Talk?" Maria Esther says. "About what? All I can talk about is the suffering I've seen. You can see how we sleep, how we live."

Late one afternoon, Chisola sits against the courtyard wall, wrapped to the chin against her malaria. In the center of the yard an energetic woman with a baby on her back claps her hands for attention and arranges about three dozen women, all Zaireans, into the rough equivalent of a chorus line. Someone has got out a drum, and the woman soon choreographs the line into a clapping and whirling routine that has only a few rough edges. It's a practice for Africa Refugee Day, not a celebration of their status exactly, but an affirmation that the UN has named a day for them, that someone knows they exist. The day won't change their lives, but it breaks the monotony with a rare burst of color and music.

The director kicks Chisola's daughter Paulina out of the line – this routine is for Zaireans only, she says. A quarrel breaks out, and Chisola, from her spot against the back wall, ends it with a few quiet words. Paulina slips back into the dancing, at the rear.

The songs are in Swahili, and Chisola sings along. Her own languages are Luwale and Chokwe, but she learned Swahili as a child in Zaire. Did she ever dance?

"Yes, I used to, but then I became a Christian and I stopped."

As the concert picks up pace, she sways with the music and it's clear that religion has little to do with her decision. Reluctantly, she admits that she would dance again, if she ever got an artificial leg.

"But I think that's impossible."

Just before noon one Monday morning, Sapassa Gosmão, one of Chisola's neighbors at the railway camp, set off on his bicycle for Luena airport. Propping his bike against a tree, the sixty-three-year-old woodseller walked into the treacherous perimeter to search for twigs and branches. Eight hundred meters from the end of the runway, he stepped on an antipersonnel mine that blew off his lower right leg.

As he called for help, he fashioned a tourniquet from the bark of a tree branch. Frantic with pain and fear, Gosmão looked up to find that his problem had suddenly worsened. The explosion had set fire to dried grass and turned the field into an inferno. To escape the spreading flames, he crawled deeper into the minefield.

Two women and a twelve-year-old boy on an adjacent path heard the blast and Gosmão's screams and ran for help. As they reached the main road, Steve Priestley was driving past on the way to Canhengue. They flagged him down, and Priestley sped off to collect a medic and a clearance team.

Nearly an hour later and as close as they could get by road, Priestley and the deminers began methodically clearing a path to the wounded man, now deep in the unmarked minefield. Sweeping and probing up the track, they found two trip wires connected to fragmentation mines and disarmed them. They could hear Gosmão's cries but couldn't see him and began yelling back to keep Gosmão talking. If he lost consciousness, they'd never find him in the dense underbrush. Weakly, Gosmão called out that he was hot and thirsty.

When they found him, the medic could not administer first aid until checking under his body in case he was lying on still another device. Running in relays, Priestley and the engineers carried him by stretcher more than two kilometers (a mile and a half) out of the minefield.

Just after two o'clock, burned and wounded but still conscious, Gosmão was carried into the hospital. His leg was amputated later that afternoon.

It was not the first time Gosmão had gone to collect firewood near the airport. He knew all the approaches were mined and knew several other people who had been wounded doing the same thing.

Later, Priestley asked him why he had gone into the fields anyway. Gosmão replied: "Because of hunger."

The cocktail party.

As two well-dressed men exchanged cordialities and small talk at a social reception one evening in Geneva, the conversation turned to their respective professions. One man was a doctor, the other a businessman with a manufacturing concern in a Western European country. As the conversation progressed, the businessman let it be known that his company was in the defense industry and that he designed antipersonnel mines for use by his country's armed forces. He considered that his occupation was making an important contribution to his country's national defense and thus an honorable contribution to society.

"I believe," the man said, neither bravado nor defensiveness in his voice, "that if there is a day of judgment, I will get into heaven."

The doctor, whose experience as a surgeon had put him in a position to speak with authority, politely replied that this particular military technology was not *always* used for national defense and sometimes fell into irresponsible hands, causing terrible suffering to people who were not a threat to the man's country.

The businessman, whose smile seemed to freeze, wished the doctor all the best in his endeavors, terminated the conversation, and walked away.

One evening halfway through the dry season and my last evening in Luena, I sat outside the Mines Advisory Group house with a mug of tea, watching the sun go down as the land gave up the day's heat. The air was sweet and dry like a Northern Hemisphere fall, small golden leaves clung to the locust trees in the park, a few pale purple blooms to the high branches of the jacarandas.

On evenings like that, and in the early mornings, Angola's misery seemed to recede, at least from my privileged vantage point. Women walked by carrying tubs of washing and firewood and bags of vegetables, a few men glided past on bicycles, and children walked hand in hand, shyly calling, "Amigo."

From down near the market, a woman with one leg and a baby on her back was walking up the sun-warm road. She took long strides on the crutches, was barefoot, and wore a yellow T-shirt and black and yellow *chitengi*. From a distance she looked like Chisola.

The woman covered ground quickly, but her steps were awkward and labored. The hand grips on her crutches were too low, keeping her bent from the waist even when she stopped. Each time the crutches touched the ground, she propelled her lower body out in front in a wide arc, something like a yard swing. Every twenty meters or so she stopped to hitch up the baby, who kept slipping down her back.

As she got closer and paused to rewrap the baby again, she looked at me briefly, a flat direct look with no discernible expression, then continued down the road and across the yellow dusty park and disappeared in the darkening trees.

Sometime after midnight, the hymns for the dead began again and echoed across town until the sun came up.

Epilogue

International agencies continued to make artificial limbs, crutches, and wheelchairs for land mine victims in several countries.

In Angola's Moxico Province, the Vietnam Veterans of America Foundation set up its prosthesis workshop, planning to produce more than two thousand plastic legs and one thousand pairs of crutches and braces over four years with the help of a $3 million grant from the U.S. Agency for International Development. Medico International expanded its program to provide assistance to the disabled, including former soldiers and children, with funding from the government of Germany.

In Afghanistan, the ICRC budgeted more than $1 million for orthopedic rehabilitation for one year.

The International Campaign to Ban Landmines and its coordinator, Jody Williams, were awarded the 1997 Nobel Peace Prize. The Campaign, hundreds of private groups, and the government of Canada maintained pressure to do away with antipersonnel mines. In December 1997 in Ottawa, more than 120 countries signed a treaty banning the manufacture, stockpiling, use and sale of these weapons. Russia, China, India, and the United States were among countries that did not sign. The Clinton administration said that U.S. forces must retain antipersonnel mines, principally to protect South Korea from an attack by North Korea, but said it would support an eventual global ban negotiated by the Conference on Disarmament in Geneva. The United States was widely criticized for its stance.

MAG, the highest-paying mine clearance charity in Angola, trimmed paychecks to $200 a month from $300 to bring local salaries closer to those of other groups. Angolan deminers briefly went on strike to protest the cuts, but returned to work. The Angolan government was said to be still planning to impose a 20 percent social insurance tax.

João Mimoso, our one-time guide on the road to Canage, was not hired by MAG. He continued his private forays to salvage parts from blown-up trucks and started a taxi service to ferry local traders between Luena and Canage. The next February, as he pulled off the road south of the N'Dala River crossing to let another vehicle pass, he drove over an antitank mine, which killed him and three other people and wounded six more.

MAG suffered its first casualty since beginning operations in Angola. Fernando Capalo, a thirty-year-old engineer, was working in a part of the old battlefield at Sangondo; confusion occurred over which part of the field had been swept, and Capalo walked into an uncleared section and stepped on a mine. For a time after the amputation, Capalo gave up the will to live and stopped eating. Through a period of acute psychological and physical stress, MAG personnel fed him daily until he was able to get out of bed and walk on crutches. MAG paid him $4,500 in insurance and offered him a less strenuous job. However, Capalo said that as soon as he can be fitted with an artificial leg, he wants to return to the minefields.

MAG continued to survey land and destroy the weapons in Angola, putting additional teams in the field and preparing to clear mines near Luau on the Zaire border when funds became available from the European Union and the United Nations High Commissioner for Refugees. Other MAG teams operated awareness centers in refugee camps in Zaire and Zambia and continued demining operations in Laos, Cambodia, and northern Iraq.

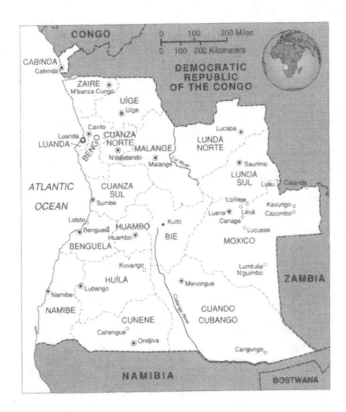

Notes

X LUCKIEST SURVIVOR IN THE WORLD

1. Africa Watch, a division of Human Rights Watch, *Land Mines in Angola*, (1993), 37.

xi NOT WAR, BUT MURDER

1. The caltrop is also a plant whose fruit pod has protective spikes.
2. Hans Delbrück, *Geschichte der Kriegkunst im Rahmen der Politischen Geschichte* (History of the Art of War within the Framework of Political History) (Berlin, 1920). Translation by Walter J. Renfroe, Jr. (Westport, CT: Greenwood Press, 1985), vol. 4, 24.
3. Milton F. Perry, *Infernal Machines: The Story of Confederate Submarine and Mine Warfare* (Louisiana State University Press, 1965), 23.
4. Ibid.
5. Ibid., 199–201.
6. Ibid., 21.
7. Ibid., 186–187.
8. Ibid., 180.
9. Burke Davis, *Sherman's March* (New York: Random House, 1980), 94–95.
10. *William Tecumseh Sherman: Memoirs of W. T. Sherman* (New York: Library of America, 1990), 670.
11. *The Civil War Papers of George B. McClellan, Selected Correspondence 1860–1865*, ed. Stephen W. Sears (New York: Ticknor and Fields, 1989), 254.
12. Perry, *Infernal Machines*, 25.
13. Lloyd Lewis, *Sherman: Fighting Prophet* (Harcourt, Brace & World, 1932). Sherman quoted on 462.

14. Perry, *Infernal Machines*, 187.

15. United States Department of State, Bureau of Political-Military Affairs, Office of International Security and Peacekeeping Operations, *Hidden Killers: The Global Landmine Crisis*, Department of State Publication 10225 (December 1994): 4–5.

16. The Arms Project, a division of Human Rights Watch, and Physicians for Human Rights, *Landmines: A Deadly Legacy* (1993), 17.

17. Eric Prokosch, *The Technology of Killing: A Military and Political History of Antipersonnel Weapons* (London: Zed Books, 1995), 109–110. For the Proxmire quote, Prokosch cites Paul Dickson, *The Electronic Battlefield* (Indiana University Press, 1976), 103.

18. "Pakistan Ordnance Factories, Technical Specifications for Mine Antipersonnel (P4 MK2)," quoted in The Arms Project, *Landmines: A Deadly Legacy*, 95.

19. United States Department of State, *Hidden Killers*, 5.

20. Ibid., 7.

21. Ibid., 7.

22. Bernard E. Trainor, article in the *New York Times* (March 28, 1996).

23. Quoted in *Deadly Legacy*, 339.

24. Colonel David H. Hackworth and Julie Sherman, *About Face* (Macmillan Company of Australia Pty Ltd, 1989). (NOTE: This quote is from the 1991 edition, published by Pan Books Ltd., London, 148.)

25. Ibid., 150.

26. *Newsweek* (April 8, 1996).

27. Ibid.

28. Ibid.

29. U.S. Defense Intelligence Agency and U.S. Army Foreign Science and Technology Center, *Landmine Warfare – Trends & Projections* DST-1160S-019-92 (December 1992), 5–1. Quoted in *Deadly Legacy*, op. cit., 45. The DIA document was obtained by the Arms Project of Human Rights Watch under the Freedom of Information Act.

1. Quoted in International Committee of the Red Cross, *Landmines Must Be Stopped* (Geneva, 1995): 7.

2. The one-year export moratorium was introduced by Senator Patrick Leahy and signed into law by President Bush in 1992. Congress has extended the moratorium through 2000, and President Clinton has said he will seek to make it permanent.

3. Leahy statement, May 16, 1996.

4. "An Open Letter to President Clinton," sponsored by the Vietnam Veterans of America Foundation, *New York Times* (April 3, 1996).

5. Austria, Benin, Canada, Cape Verde, Croatia, France, Ghana, Germany, India, Jordan, Netherlands, Norway, Peru, Philippines, Slovenia, South Africa, Switzerland, United Kingdom, and Zimbabwe.

6. International Committee of the Red Cross, *Anti-personnel Landmines: Friend or Foe? A study of the military use and effectiveness of antipersonnel mines,* (Geneva, March 1996).

7. Bernard E. Trainor, article in the *New York Times* (March 28, 1996).

8. Flyer reprinted in U.S. Department of State, Bureau of Political-Military Affairs, Office of International Security Operations, *Hidden Killers: The Global Problem with Uncleared Landmines,* (July 1993).

Acknowledgments

Many people helped with this book, and if I have neglected to name any of them, I hope they'll excuse the oversight. All graciously gave information and considerable time in dealing with a reporter's endless questions. Several people frequently risked their own safety and security to assist me, and I am grateful to them.

Special thanks to two excellent journalists: Chris Simpson of the BBC and Nicholas Shaxson of Reuters got me hooked on Angola, generously shared hard-collected information, and helped me out on more occasions that I can count. David Shad, Janse Sörman, and Sandra Legg of the World Food Program got me onto the airplanes with unfailing civility, even when they were under enormous pressure moving emergency supplies; the Transafrik and other cargo pilots always got me to my destination and back. All the people of the Mines Advisory Group, former and present, helped with logistics: Chris MacKenzie and Graeme Goldsworthy in the U.K., and Catherine Allen in Luanda. In Luena, Dave Turner, Steve Priestly, and David Rice did the same and gave me unlimited access and time, as did the Angolan deminers, and, of course, Rae and Lou McGrath.

On trips to Angola between 1993 and 1996, Katia Airola, Eduardo Minvu, Benedito Diogo, Diamantino Doba, and Vita Matundo provided invaluable support on many occasions and devoted plenty of time to making sure I got where I needed to go, often at inconvenient hours.

Dozens of people in nongovernmental organizations and relief agencies contributed to this book by making me welcome and making sure I understood the story. UN peacekeepers and field workers of Concern, Médecins sans Frontières, the International Committee of the Red

Cross, the World Food Program, and others habitually risk their own lives to help war victims and get little thanks for doing so. Mike McDonagh and Isabel Simpson are among them.

Robin Coupland, Peter Herby, and Johanne Dorais-Slakmon of the ICRC in Geneva assisted in reviewing legal and medical matters.

Alex Vines of Human Rights Watch U.K. shared valuable sources over the years. Jody Williams and Mary Wareham of the Campaign and Steve Goose and Andrew Cooper of the Arms Project of Human Rights Watch patiently provided information. Lt. Col. Steve Ransley, Kevin Cassidy, and Mary Fowler at the UN always made themselves available, as did Eddie and Pat Banks.

Valuable guidance came from Hans Husum of Trauma Care in Norway and from Hans Birkeland of the Norwegian government.

These people also contributed: Susan Walker of Handicap International, Barbara Ayotte of Physicians for Human Rights, Hap Hambric, Bill Arkin, Michael Qualls, and Lesley Carson. I would like to thank three good friends: Denise Chong, Canadian author, was of particular help and encouraged me from the start; the late Jarlath Dolan, an Irish newspaperman, reminded me by energetic example that telling human stories is a privileged occupation; and Stephen Handelman, journalist and author, provided lots of valuable advice.

Special thanks to Sharon Basco, who urged me to write the book and supported me throughout. This project would not have happened without her.

Finally, the people who made the book: When I once visited a remote village in Northeastern Angola, Chokwe-speaking villagers had no word for "journalist," so my translator had to invent one. Rendered back into English, it came out roughly as "the white people who come and ask lots of questions and then go away again." Time and again, Angolan civilians, many of them badly wounded and left destitute by the war, put up with my questions and photographs. None of them were any better off when I went away again, and I thank them for their time and their courage.